Christian Theology in African Context

Essential Writings of Eshetu Abate

Samuel Yonas Deressa, editor

Lutheran University Press
Minneapolis, Minnesota

Christian Theology in African Context
Essential Writings of Eshetu Abate
Samuel Yonas Deressa, editor

Copyright © 2015 Lutheran University Press, an imprint of 1517 Media. All rights reserved. Except for brief quotations in articles or reviews, no part of this book may be reproduced in any manner without written permission of the publisher: 1517 Media Permissions, PO Box 1209, Minneapolis, MN 55440-1209, or copyright@1517.media.

Published under the auspices of Evangelical Mekane Yesus Lutheran Fellowship in North America

ISBN: 978-1-942304-09-8
eISBN: 978-1-942304-50-0

Contents

Foreword 5

Introduction 9

The Church, Culture, and Ethnicity: A Theological View 17

Human Sexuality and AIDS:

An Ethiopian Church Perspective 29

Battle for Justification by Faith in the African Context 41

The Theology of the Cross in the African Context 57

Confessing Christ in the Apostles' Creed 81

Christian Faith in the New Millennium 99

Foreword

Before acknowledging those who have directly or indirectly contributed for the publication of this book, I would like to state briefly about the Evangelical Mekane Yesus Lutheran Fellowship in North America and Europe (EMYLFNA). The EMYLFNA was founded ten years ago by Ethiopian evangelical believers living in America on July 22, 2005, at Concordia University in Irvine, California. The Rev. Dr. Eshetu was the one who called on the meeting, convincingly argued for the importance of establishing the fellowship, and proposed how the fellowship could successfully carry out its God-given task (mission) in the context of the new millennium. Eshetu was then elected as the first chairman, and he served on this position until he passed away on December 28, 2011.

In the last ten years, congregations were planted under EMYLFNA in Maryland, Virginia; Washington D.C.; Columbus, Ohio; Sioux Falls, South Dakota; Seattle, Washington; Nashville, Tennessee; Memphis, Tennessee; St. Paul, Minnesota; Cary, North Carolina; Jacksonville, Florida; Irvine, California; and Schaumburg, Illinois. Under the leadership of highly experienced men and women of God, this fellowship has come to the point where we have started to see, enjoy, and witness the purpose of God being materialized in our congregations. Through a television and radio broadcast named *Yemeserach Dimtse*, the EMYLFNA has been addressing the Christians in Africa (including Ethiopia), Europe, and North America.

The EMYLFNA also works in partnership with the home church, the Ethiopian Evangelical Church Mekane Yesus (EECMY). There have been seminars and forums organized by the EECMY and the EMYLFNA to strengthen the partnership between the two, and common goals have been identified as areas where the two can work in partnership. In the United States, EMYLFNA has already signed partnership with the North American Lutheran Church (NALC), and aims to partner and work with other mission organizations in the future.

With this publication, the EMYLFNA begins to address one of the needs of churches in Africa, which is to publish books that are of significant contribution to the wider Christian community in Africa and beyond. To begin with Eshetu's works is the right choice we have made. The pages that follow give evidence of Eshetu's careful research and well-balanced perspective. This book will be treasured as a memento for those of us who knew Eshetu personally, and those who had the opportunity to be his students at Mekane Yesus Seminary, Ethiopian Graduate School of Theology, and Concordia University in Irvine, California.

First of all, I thank God for his gift of such a humble and dedicated leader and pastor who happened to be also a prolific theologian—Eshetu Abate. I pray this book will contribute to flourishing churches in Africa and beyond. To God be all the glory, now and forever. It is also a deep honor now to thank a young theologian, Samuel Yonas Deressa, who has worked hard as an editor of this book to make sure that Eshetu's work are presented this way. I thank the Lutheran University Press for showing interest to publish this book. I also thank Eshetu's wife, Amarech Getachew, for giving us the permission to publish Eshetu's essays.

Finally, thank you to my colleagues and board members (and also advisory board members and board chaplain) of the EMYLFNA. The board members are: Rev. Dr. Tilahun Mendedo,

Rev. Dr. Yared Halche, Ato Teodros Workneh, Rev. Dr. Gemechis Buba, Mrs. Bruktawit Assefa, Ato Behailu Estifanos, Dr. Haimanot Ze-Amanuel, and Ato Solomon Damtew. The advisory board members are: Rev. Francis Stephanos, Mr. Endalkachew Kidanewold, and the board chaplain Rev. Tesfaye Dinagde. I consider it a privilege indeed to serve with each of you. We share the special gift of collegiality in a remarkable way.

Rev. Dr. Alemseged A. Hagos, EMYLFNA board chair person

Introduction

"The Christian faith begins by grace,
exists by grace, and comes to fulfillment by grace."
Eshetu Abate, in *African Bible Commentary*

This book is a collection of Rev. Dr. Eshetu Abate's essays originally published in different books and journals. The significance of the essays for churches in Ethiopia and beyond can be described in two ways. First, they were written during the last period of the Socialist government of Ethiopia and the first decade of the Federal Democratic Republic of Ethiopia (between 1990 and 2002). This time signifies the years in which Ethiopia was going through social, economic, political, and religious changes. Eshetu, as a prominent theologian and pastor, reflects on issues that the Ethiopian communities faced during those periods. Second, Eshetu is one among few Ethiopian theologians who have initiated the conversation about Christian theology from an African perspective. He understood his own context, which included the crucial, existential issues that African Christians were facing, to be the legitimate context out of which Christian theology should emerge. He did so without compromising the centeredness and uniqueness of Christ.

The idea to publish Eshetu's works occurred to me and leaders of the Evangelical Mekane Yesus Lutheran Fellowship in North America (EMYLFNA) a few months ago while we were disusing how Ethiopian theologians living in America and Europe might be able to contribute to theological developments in

Ethiopia and beyond. This idea was further accelerated and fueled by the intense interest that the Ethiopian Evangelical Church Mekane Yesus (EECMY) leaders and theologians showed on having Eshetu's works available for theological schools and pastors in Ethiopia.

I knew Eshetu personally while he was teaching at Mekane Yesus Seminary (MYS). He and my father, Yonas Deressa, were close friends and coworkers. Both of them had lectured in the same institution for years. They were also part-time pastors at the Addis Ababa Mekane Yesus congregation. I was attending elementary and high school while the two labored together. Eshetu left Ethiopia and joined Concordia University in Irvine, California, in 2002, a year before I became a student at MYS for my first degree in theology. It was at MYS that I was first introduced to some of his essays by one of my professors, Rev. Dr. Johnny Bakke. Few years later, lecturing at MYS (2008-2011); I included these essays as part of the required readings for one course on African Christian Theology. I also had the opportunity to have fruitful conversations with Eshetu about his essays and some other theological issues when he visited me and my siblings during his trip to Ethiopia for a vacation in 2008. I found Eshetu to be a man of deep theological knowledge. He was humble and generous in his personality, and creative and visionary in his leadership.

For me personally the publication of Eshetu's essays comes as complement to another project about one of our church's most notable leader. Since 2007 I have been engaged in coordinating the publications of Gudina Tumsa's writings and the proceedings of Seminars and forums held to perpetuate his legacy. Gudina was the General Secretary of the EECMY (1966-1979) whose life was snuffed by the Socialist government of Ethiopia on July 28, 1979, due to his prophetic voice against injustice. Many theologians in the West and Africa describe Gudina as the Dietrich Bonhoeffer of Africa.[1] Gudina was a theologian, prolific writer, charismatic leader, and political figure who made an immense contributions to African Christianity. His writings and legacy are of great significance to the global Christian community.[2]

Friends from Africa and other parts of the world who have been asking if there exist any other Ethiopian leader and/or theologians beside Gudina who has made similar contributions to Christianity in Africa. In response, many of us are agreed that the time has come to consider the writings and the legacy of another Ethiopian theologian and leader, Eshetu of the EECMY. Eshetu is different from Gudina in many ways. Gudina served many of his years leading the church while Eshetu was a lecturer with a minimal leadership. Gudina's writings were solely addressed to churches in Ethiopia and beyond and were not intended for academic consumption; Eshetu's essays, on the other hand, were published primarily for theological study. Gudina's theology is ho-

---

1   Paul Wee, "Dietrich Bonhoeffer and Gudina Tumsa: Shaping the Church's Response to the Challenge of our Day," in *Church and Society*, 15-52; Gerd Decke, "Gudina Tumsa and Dietrich Bonhoeffer," in *Emerging Theological Praxis: Journal of Gudina Tumsa Theological Forum*, Samuel Yonas Deressa, ed. (Minneapolis: Lutheran University Press, 2011), 23-55.
2   Paul E. Hoffman, ed., *The Life and Ministry of Gudina Tumsa, General Secretary of the Ethiopian Evangelical Church Mekane Yesus* (Hamburg: WDL Publishers, 2008). *Church and Society:* Paul E. Hoffman, ed., *Lectures and Responses on the Life and Ministry of Gudina Tumsa*, (Hamburg: WDL-Publisher, 2010). Habtamu Bula, *"The Church Should Be a Voice of the Voiceless": A Short Biography of the Reverend Gudina Tumsa* (Addis Ababa: Mekane Yesus Seminary, B.Th. paper 1995). Øyvind M. Eide, "Gudina Tumsa: The Voice of an Ethiopian Prophet," *Svensk Missions Tidskrift* 89/3 (2001). *Contemporary Theological Perspectives: Journal of Gudina Tumsa Theological Forum* (Addis Ababa: Gudina Tumsa Foundation, 2011); *Emerging Theological Praxis: Journal of Gudina Tumsa Theological Forum* (Minneapolis: Lutheran University Press, 2012); *Ecumenical Challenges: Working in Love, Transforming Lives; Journal of Gudina Tumsa Theological Forum* (Minneapolis: Lutheran University Press, 2013).

listic in nature, which Øyvind Eide described as a theology of "love and justice,"³ while Eshetu's essays are about the relevance and applicability of Christian theology in African socio-cultural contexts.

Gudina and Eshetu are also similar in some ways: In the first place, they were both concerned about the socio-economic condition in Ethiopia, and therefore attempted to respond from theological perspectives. Secondly, both lived in similar contexts, which impacted their theology, during the feudal (up to 1974) and socialist governments (1974-1991) of Ethiopia. Eshetu also lived during the period of the federal government (1991 to present) until his death on December 2011. Thirdly, they are both Christ-centered in their theological approach. They both had the conviction that a Christian or the church should evaluate and face realities from the perspective of the cross of Jesus Christ.

Eshetu was a theological thinker, pastor, and a leader of considerable reputation. Through his lectures and writings, he has contributed to the development of theology in an African context. In his leadership and life testimony; he was able to influence his students, who later became leaders in different churches and organizations throughout the world. Eshetu died of cancer on December 28, 2011, in California.

Eshetu was born in 1955 to his mother, Ijigayehu Kasaye, and his father, Abate Koyra, in the *Arbe Gona* district of *Sidama Zone* in the southern part of Ethiopia. He completed his primary and secondary school education at *Sodo* town of *Wollaita* in 1974. Though he was offered the opportunity to study medicine in the Soviet Union, he insisted on studying theology and follow-

---

3 Øyvind M. Eide, "Integral Human Development," in *The Life and Ministry of Gudina Tumsa*, 38. See also Paul E. Hoffman, "'Ministry to the Whole Man' Revisited—A Look Back in Order to Look Ahead," in *Serving the Whole Person: The Practice and Understanding of Diakonia Within the Lutheran Communion*, ed. Kjell Schlagenhaft (Minneapolis: Lutheran University Press, 2009).

ing God's call. He earned his Bachelor of Theology degree from Mekane Yesus Seminary in Addis Ababa in 1981, and his Ph.D. from Concordia Seminary in Saint Louis, Missouri, in 1988.

He served as a teacher and vice principal at the Tabour Mekane Yesus Seminary in Hawassa (1981-1983). When Tabour Seminary was confiscated by the former Marxist Government of Ethiopia, he was called to Mekane Yesus Seminary, where he served as a teacher and academic dean of the Department of Theology (1988-1992), and as principal (1996-2000). He was one of the visionaries that started the Ethiopian Graduate School of Theology, where he lectured for two years (1994-1996). In the meantime, he was called by the Addis Ababa Mekane Yesus Congregation to ordained ministry and served the congregation on a voluntary basis. He has also served at the Bible Society of Ethiopia as consultant for Bible translation.

Eshetu was a lecturer at Concordia University in Irvine, California, as member of Christ College's faculty from 2002 untill his death. Besides teaching, he was engaged in planting congregations for Ethiopian Lutherans living in America. These congregations were planted in Los Angeles and in Long Beach. He was among the founders and chairperson of the EMYLFNA which was founded by the members of the EECMY in North America. He also led the team and contributed to the peace and reconciliation process between the EECMY and the congregations that separated from the Church for over twelve years (the so-called Addis Ababa and the Surrounding Church).

Eshetu's contribution to theological development in Africa has not been given due consideration. His contributions include a commentary on the books of Philippians and Titus in *Africa Bible Commentary* (where he made a remark that "[t]he Christian faith begins by grace, exists by grace, and comes to fulfillment by grace"); "A Study Note" in *The Lutheran Study Bible* published by Lutheran Church–Missouri Synod (LCMS); Amharic books on the *Trinity and Sacraments*, and many others. His unpublished dissertation is entitled *The Apostolic Tradition: A study of the texts and origins, and its Eucharistic teachings with a special exploration of the Ethiopic version.*[4]

There are six essays included in this publication. The editor decided on their order based on their content rather than their chronological order. The essays are: "The Church, Culture and Ethnicity: A Theological View,"[5] "Human Sexuality and Aids: An Ethiopian Church Perspective,"[6] "Battle for Justification by Faith in the African Context,"[7] "The Theology of the Cross in the African Context,"[8] "Confessing the Christ of the Apostles' Creed,"[9] and "Christian Faith in the New Millenium."

There are many people and institutions that I need to thank for their contribution in the publication of this book. This publication would be impossible without the permission from institutions that first published Eshetu's essays: Concordia Publishing House, *Evangelical Reviews of Theology, Word and World, Concordia Journal*, and the East African Educational Publishers. I would like to

---

4 Eshetu Abate, *The Apostolic Tradition: A study of the texts and origins, and its Eucharistic teachings with a special exploration of the Ethiopic version* (Th. D. Thesis, Concordia Seminary 1988).
5 This article was first published in *Evangelical Review of Theology* 24:2, 2000, and now reprinted with permission from *Paternoster Periodical*.
6 This article originally appeared in *Word & World* 21/2 (2001): 152-159. Copyright © 2001 *Word & World*. Used with permission.
7 This article was first published in *Concordia Journal of October 1999*. Used with permission.
8 Eshetu Abate, "The theology of the cross in the African context" in *The Theology of the Cross for the 21st Century: Signposts for a Multicultural Witness* (St. Louis: Concordia, 2002). Used with permission.
9 Eshetu Abate, "Confessing the Christ of the Apostles' Creed" in *And Every Tongue Confess: Essays in honor of Norman Nagel on the occasion of his sixty-fifth birthday* (Dearborn, Michigan: Nagel Festschrift Committee, 1990); "Confessing Christ in the Apostles' Creed" in *Issues in African Christian Theology* (Nairobi: East African Educational Publishers, 1998). Published with permission.

also thank Luther Seminary librarian Karen Alexander for helping me trace and obtain copies of Eshetu's essays from other libraries.

The deepest thanks go to Karen Walhof, Lutheran University Press, for her support and willingness to publish these valuable works of Eshetu. Special mention must be made of the contribution made by EMYLFNA board members: Rev. Dr. Tilahun Mendedo, Rev. Dr. Yared Halche, Ato Teodros Workneh, Rev. Dr. Gemechis Buba, Mrs. Bruktawit Assefa, Ato Behailu Estifanos, Dr. Haimanot Ze-Amanuel and Ato Solomon Damtew. For all that contributed in one way or another, I would like to say thank you for assuring that Eshetu's legacy will endure for us and for generations to come.

Samuel Yonas Deressa, editor

The Church, Culture, and Ethnicity: A Theological View

The church is the body of Christ. Like her Lord she has two natures, the supernatural and the natural. She shares in the supernatural (the spiritual) because of her unique access and relationship to her heavenly Lord and the natural because she exists and operates in the natural world.

It is not new for the church of Jesus Christ to operate within cultures and ethnic groups. It has done this from the very inception of the church. In fact, the founder of the church, our Lord Jesus Christ, did his mission within a certain culture and ethnic group. His great commission was "to disciple all nations [all ethnic groups], baptizing them in the name of the Father, the Son, and the Holy Spirit. . . ." The apostles, obeying the commission of our Lord, went with the gospel to all parts of the known world of that time, thus reaching all ethnic and cultural groups.

This means that the church today is not starting from scratch. We, as the church, have models to follow—our Lord Jesus Christ and his apostles—in our dealings with culture and ethnicity. Besides, his promise in the great commission to be with his church to "the very end of the age" assures his continued guidance throughout her ministry on this earth. Thus the church, guided by his Word and Spirit, can get directions on how to deal with different cultures and ethnic groups. Nevertheless, in the history of missions it has not been as easy to put this into practice as it should be.

Before we look at some theological models for the church's interaction with culture and ethnicity, let us see briefly what characteristics the church, culture, and an ethnic group have.

The Church

In his book *Know the Truth*, Bruce Milne lists four important characteristics of the true church. The first of these is *unity*. The true church is characterized by its unity. Unity, however, does not mean total uniformity. Though the basic theological conviction is one, it could be expressed in different ways. Worship is done in the one Spirit to the one God, though forms may vary from place to place. Where possible, Christians who confess the same apostolic gospel should demonstrate their oneness in faith in their visible relationships. Milne writes:

> The New Testament addressed its teaching on unity to specific Christian groups with immediate implications for their visible relationships. . . . In other words, there is need to search for a fuller visible unity than is presently experienced among those who confess the apostolic gospel. . . . The deepest challenge of this teaching, however, is at the level of relationships in a local church. In that setting the unity of life in Christ should express itself in genuine and tangible care for, and commitment to, one another. In default of this the claim to be an authentic Christian church is called into question.[1]

The second mark of a true church is *holiness*. The character of holiness is the result of the union of the church and its members with Christ, so that it may be said, "A church which is a stranger to holiness is a stranger to Christ." Having said that, we have to admit that the New Testament presents a picture of

---

1 Bruce Milne, *Know the Truth* (Leicester: Inter-Varsity Press, 1982), 216.

churches marked with division, error, sin, and other limitations. Nevertheless, some visible degree of holiness has to be seen in a true church of God.

The third mark of a true church is its *catholicity* or *universality*. One distinguishing characteristic of the early church was its openness to all. Judaism and other sectarian movements of the time were not. Milne writes,

> The key aspect of the early church's catholicity was its openness to all. In distinction from Judaism with its racial exclusivism and Gnosticism with its intellectual and cultic exclusivism, the church opened its arms to all who would hear its message and embrace its savior, irrespective of color, race, social status, intellectual capacity or moral history. It broke upon the world as a faith for all. . . . Churches which erect other "tests" should be viewed with suspicion. There is no place in a true church for racial, color, social, intellectual, or moral discrimination, provided in the last-mentioned case there is evidence of true repentance.[2]

The fourth mark of a true church is its *apostolicity*. The church is built on the foundations of the apostles and prophets, with Christ Jesus himself as the chief cornerstone (Ephesians 2:20). Apostolicity does not mean for us an historic continuity of bishops that goes back in succession to the first apostles and Christ, but conformity to the apostolic faith.

Culture

In comparison with the other lower animals, only human beings have cultures. This separates human beings from the lower animals. As usual there is no single definition of culture which is

---
2 Ibid., 218.

accepted by all. One definition given to culture is "the integrated system of learned patterns of behavior, ideas and products characteristic of a society."[3] Sir Edward Tylor, the pioneer British anthropologist, gave the following classical definition of culture. According to him culture is "that complex whole which includes knowledge, belief, art, morals, law, custom, and any other capabilities and habits acquired by man as a member of society."[4]

Ethnicity

People belonging to an ethnic group have certain factors by which they distinguish themselves from others. First of all, one belongs to an ethnic group by birth. Because of this a feeling and consciousness of kinship is common among members of a particular ethnic group. Ethnic identity is not based as much on a common culture as on a common sense of identity which is expressed in certain cultural values and symbols such as language. To maintain these signs and symbols is essential to the survival of the group as a distinct body and to symbolize its identity to others.

The Interaction of the Church with Cultures and Ethnic Groups

The Incarnational Model

The incarnational model is the one which was chosen by the creator himself. When he came to the world he took our flesh. To be specific, he took not the flesh of anybody but the flesh of Mary who lived in a certain geographical location (Palestine) and historical time (around 4 B.C.). He had to grow as a Galilean Jew. He knew the Aramaic language, including the proverbs of his people. In a way the limitless Word limited or accommodat-

---

[3] Paul G. Hiebert, *Cultural Anthropology* (Grand Raids: Baker, 1983), 25.
[4] Stephen A. Grunlan and Marvin K. Mayers, *Cultural Anthropology* (Grand Rapids: Zondervan, 1988), 39.

ed himself to the Jewish culture and people. In fact his was a complete immersion in and identification with the culture. This model points to the fact that no one is more suited to be a missionary or to lead a local church than the person from the local culture. One problem the church has faced through the ages is in her cross-cultural evangelization. This is partly due to lack of indigenous people who can do the job, and partly due to the belief that no one else can do better than the cross-cultural evangelist.

Our Lord Jesus Christ gave the challenge of cross-cultural communication to his apostles when he gave the great commission. As we stated above, the apostles obeyed the commission. The Apostle Paul understood very clearly the incarnational model the gospel of Jesus Christ takes as it moves from culture to culture and from an ethnic group to another. Two instances in his letters show this fact clearly. First, when writing to the Corinthians, he explained:

> Though I am free and belong to no man, I make myself a slave to everyone, to win as many as possible. To the Jews I became like a Jew, to win the Jews. To those under the law, I became like one under the law (though I myself am not under the law) so as to win those under the law. . . . I have become all things to all men so that by all possible means I might save some (1 Corinthians 9:19-23).

Then again in the reference to the dispute over the place of the Jewish law, he said,

> When I saw that they were not acting in line with the truth of the gospel, I said to Peter in front of them all. "You are a Jew, yet you live like a Gentile and not like a Jew. How is it, then, that you force Gentiles to follow Jewish customs?" (Galatians 2:14).

The Apostle Paul believed that one did not need to forsake or leave one's own culture or custom to be a Christian. One can come as one is.

The cultural barrier between the evangelist and the hearers which often exists is one of the reasons why people do not understand and therefore accept the Christian gospel. Sahdu Sundar Singh, an Indian evangelist who preached the gospel to his own people as a Hindu *Sahdu* (holy man), once said, "When the water of life is given with an European cup, most of my people refused to drink, however now when it is given with the familiar Indian cup they run to drink and quench their thirst." This is not to deny that conversion is ultimately the work of the Holy Spirit. However, one needs to remove cultural barriers that stand in the way so that the Holy Spirit may give life to the listener.

The tremendous revival that took place in southern Ethiopia in the 1940s and the recent revival during the Derg Regime all over the country are for the most part the result of an incarnational model of evangelization. The revival was accompanied mostly with songs that have taken into consideration the cultural melodies and tunes of the society.

The Message of Reconciliation Upgrades Culture and Ethnicity

Transforming Culture

The church does not embrace all elements of culture as they are. Cultural elements which contradict the spirit of the gospel have to be discarded, as the experiences of the early church at the Jerusalem Council indicate (Acts 15:19-20). Elements which do not contradict but express the identity of the group have to be maintained. The distinction between the two can best be made by the local people or Christians. In a way the church "baptizes" cultures. It consecrates the whole way of life in that culture to the Lord. The church and her evangelists most often made the mistake of dictating from the outside as to which element of the culture was biblical. Sometimes, without valuing the thought patterns of the other culture, they tried to judge on the basis of their own culture. This then becomes an ethnocentric approach.

Reconciling Cultures and Ethnic Groups

The church's message of reconciliation is the results of the cross—the death and resurrection of our Lord Jesus Christ. The church itself is the result of the cross, that is the reconciliation made available by our Lord. As people from a culture are incorporated into the church, they become a reconciled people and a people of reconciliation. We can see this from two angles.

Reconciliation with God. There is no question about this. Christ has done it all. It is finished. One has simply to make oneself available and accept the finished work. The way to God has been opened. The sin which blocked our free access to God is taken away.

Reconciliation of Ethnic Groups. It was taboo for a Jew even to associate with a Samaritan or a Gentile, quite apart from eating together. It would have made sense for an ethnic group not to associate with the other if it had a unique merit or a reason to boast. But now in the church of Jesus Christ, as we are all reconciled alike on a common basis, the death and resurrection of our Lord, we have a reason to be together as brothers and sisters. Our Lord has carried the sin of the world. That includes the sin and atrocities done by one ethnic group upon another and vice versa. If we see from the perspective of the cross and the gospel of our Lord Jesus Christ, we have no reason to be guilt ridden, nor do we have to keep on counting the guilt of others. The cross has forgiven all and removed all sins. Therefore, the former oppressor and the oppressed can come together as equals and with dignity in front of the cross. "You are all sons of God through faith in Christ Jesus, for all of you who were baptized into Christ have clothed yourselves with Christ. There is neither Jew nor Greek, slave nor free, male nor female, for you are all one in Christ Jesus" (Galatians 3:26-28). Paul G. Hiebert rightly says, "The gospel breaks down the barriers of ethnocentrism that divide people in opposing camps of Jews and Gentiles, slaves and masters, and males and females. It seeks to restore fellowship between God and humans, and between humans.[5]

This is what the church should exemplify by the brotherly love, respect, and harmonious relationship that exists between its members from different cultural and ethnic backgrounds.

We are in Christ a new community. The church forms a new community, a community of the redeemed. The ethos of this community is not the same as that from which its members came. The apostle addresses the Christian community in his time saying, "But you are a chosen people, a royal priesthood, a holy nation, a people belonging to God, that you may declare the praises of him who called you out of darkness into his wonderful light. Once you were not a people, but now you are the people of God; once you had not received mercy, but now you have received mercy" (1 Peter 2:9-10). As people of God, the new community, we have to think about things above.

The Global and Ethiopian Context
The Global Context

In the global scene the cold war ended after forty years of rivalry between the U.S.A. and the former Soviet Union. The fall of communism with the Soviet Union created a vacuum for different forces to replace it. Ninan Koshy writes:

---

[5] Hiebert, *Cultural Anthropology*, xx.

An important feature of the emerging global situation is the contest between the forces of integration and those of fragmentation. One the one hand, barriers that have historically separated nations and peoples in politics, economics, technology, and culture are breaking down. Technology and economics have become truly transnational. . . . On the other hand, forces of disintegration within nations and states are gathering momentum. Large states whose continued existence has been taken for granted have broken into pieces. New demands for nationhood—and revival of old demands—threaten many more states.[6]

To a certain extent the disorder in the international scene is caused by ethnic conflicts. The ethnic group probably has become the predominant grassroots political unit in the world today. Analysts tell us that in the last two decades ethnic conflicts have become especially widespread and that ethnicity has been at the center of politics in country after country. As such it has become a challenge to the unity of states and a cause of international tension. In the September 1998 issue of a *World Vision Newsletter*, MARC reports that there are 8,0000 identifiable separate cultural groups on earth and potentially 5,000 of them could demand the right of self-determination and creation of their own states.

One of the reasons for the explosion of ethnic conflicts on the world scene is the fact that throughout the cold war ancient cultural, ethnic, and linguistic groups remained trapped and largely separated within artificial frontiers that had been imposed upon them. In connection with this development, religion is making a growing influence in the politics of ethnic and national identi-

---

6 Ninan Koshy, *Churches in the World of Nations* (Geneva: WCC, 1994), 107-108.

ty. Sometimes situations have been created in which it has been difficult to separate a certain religion from an ethnic group and nation. For example, in the former Soviet Union, Armenians are "Christians" while the Azerbaijanis are "Muslims."

The Ethiopian Context

The Ethiopian context is not very much different from the global context. There are over eighty ethnic groups in Ethiopia. With the fall of Communism, the country has been divided administratively into fourteen regional states based primarily on ethnicity. These fourteen states are under the federal government, implying that each state has its own limited autonomy. In some circles also we hear and see ethnic revival and a desire for self-determination. It is in this context that churches of Ethiopia exercise the biblically based transformation, reconciliation, and mutual respect which we described above.

The Church as a Model of Reconciliation

The above conditions exert their influence on the churches and on the different ethnic groups who are members of the churches, either directly or indirectly. In some cases they may even result in conflicts.

The solution in such cases is to truly come to the common faith and investigate the kind of relationship that should exist in its light. As Christians, with the Apostle Paul, we should value the new community or "the new ethnicity" in the Lord more than our natural descent or relation (Philippians 3:4-11; John 1:12-13).

One of the factors that aggravates ethnic conflict within a local church is lack of transparency. According to the teaching of our Lord, there is nothing hidden which will not come to the light. Non-transparency only broods distrust and division. Therefore the churches should create an open forum for their members to discuss issues of concern and find solutions. Ethnic conflicts are one of them. Nevertheless one has to admit that it is not easy to come to a consensus because there are many conflicting forces from inside and outside the church, from above and from below. The church is not made up of only the redeemed. Our Lord likened the kingdom of God to a net that has collected both good and bad fish. In the same way we have in the church people of different backgrounds and levels of understanding.

Another factor that can help solve conflicts is negotiation. A learned anthropologist once remarked that when conflicts arise, negotiations should continue until a consensus is reached. In such situations there is no use in stopping the negotiation before a consensus is reached.

If ethnic conflicts are solved in the church, this can be a model society at large. The churches should put forward their own well-studied manifesto of ethnic relationships that can be a model for society at large to follow. The whole manifesto should center around Christ's actions in reconciling the world with his Father and with one another. There is a limitless resource in the cross and resurrection of our Lord Jesus Christ to straighten the relationships between ethnic groups and cultures. We, the Evangelical Churches of Ethiopia, together with others should very soon embark on doing that by carrying the message of reconciliation and harmony wrought in the death and resurrection of our Lord Jesus Christ.

Human Sexuality and AIDS: An Ethiopian Church Perspective

Human Sexuality in Christian Perspective

The Bible and Sexuality

According to the Christian faith, God, in the beginning, created human beings in his own image, male and female. On the basis of the creation story in the Scriptures, we can say that sexual differentiation among human beings is the will of God and derives from him. Our sexuality is the creation and gift of God.

As creatures made in the image of God, we were made with a sensitivity to what is right and wrong, holy and unholy. Thus, we have the responsibility to use our whole bodies, including our sexuality, in a responsible way. Otherwise, not knowing the purpose for which we were created, we can misuse or harm the body given to us by God.

Our God is a God of fellowship and mutuality. God created human beings as male and female because he saw such a pair to be very good. God said, "It is not good that the man should be alone; I will make him a helper as his partner" (Genesis 2:18). The one-to-one relationship that God created between Adam and Eve is the most suitable and most intimate relationship humans can have on this earth. The strength of the relationship between husband and wife and the depth of its commitment is far greater than in the relationship one has to parents ("Therefore a man leaves his father and his mother and clings to his wife, and they become one flesh"—Genesis 2:24). If the unity of the opposite sexes ("one flesh") has such a significant place in the sight of the Creator, then such union should be exercised in human communities with a full understanding of its importance and meaning.

The expression "one flesh" has another important implication. One cannot tear down one's own body or flesh. The unity, once given, cannot be broken at will. To do so will harm one's own body ("Therefore what God has joined together, let no one separate"—Matthew 19:5).

Helping each other implies unity and love, but not merely sentimental or emotional love. True love is unconditional love, sacrificial love. Our Lord said, "No one has greater love than this, to lay down one's life for one's friends" (John 15:13). The marital relationship between committed people of opposite sexes should exemplify this kind of love. An "if . . ." love loves the other person because of something one gets. In other words, it is connected with selfishness. Unconditional love on the other hand does not set a condition to love the other person. God created the sexual bond so that it could culminate in such unconditional love.

In this kind of lifelong marital bond God has allowed reproduction. It is the second purpose of God in creating human beings male and female. God said, "Be fruitful and multiply, and fill the earth. . ." (Genesis 1:28). The children born in the image of their parents look up to the parents for education and good example. In other words, the lifelong commitment between couples has its effect not only on the couple themselves but also on their children. Eventually, in fact, unfaithfulness in marriage is not only a problem of the immediate couple and their children but also a problem of the society as a whole. Therefore, societies, to be healthy and sound, should show utmost care for the stability of their families.

Christian Sexual Norms

Everybody desires to know how to behave. The Scriptures, as the word of God, give us God's own norms and directions about how to act sexually.

1. The Scriptures presuppose maturity before sexual intercourse (Genesis 2:24). Couples must be mature before they can commit themselves to one another fully. The maturity should be physical, mental, and social. According to the Scriptures a boy and girl are under the care of their "father and mother" until the time of maturity. Commitment to a person of the opposite sex in sexual relationship is right only after the time of maturity.

2. The time before maturity is the time of learning. The responsibility for teaching correct sexual behavior lies with parents, teachers, and the community at large.

3. Once the time of maturity is reached, the Scriptures endorse a one-to-one relationship between people of opposite sex as the proper setting for sexual expression. This one-to-one relationship is a lifelong commitment.

4. The Scriptures oppose extra-marital sex. Sex outside the one-to-one relationship of marriage works against the order and safety that God has created for man and woman.

5. In the Scriptures God commanded his people that they "shall not commit adultery" (Exodus 20:14). The Bible, however, does not limit adultery or sexual immorality to married people. Any intercourse that does not occur within the one-to-one commitment of marriage is contrary to the will of God. This means that married people have to remain faithfully in their marriage commitment and that unmarried single persons cannot have sexual intercourse before their marriage.

6. In the New Testament our Lord taught that divorce is permitted only for the single reason of adultery. Sexual faithfulness

between the two partners is the most important ingredient of married life. The Apostle Paul advised both married and single Christians about their sexual life. Single persons who are tempted and cannot control themselves should marry. Those who want to remain single and think they can control themselves can remain single. On the other hand, the advice of the apostle to the married is very clear: "The wife should not separate from her husband . . . the husband should not divorce his wife" (1 Corinthians 7:10-11).

7. Marriage constitutes "one body" or "one flesh" (Genesis 2:24; Matthew 19:5-6; Ephesians 5:28-31). Nobody wants his or her own body to be cut, wounded, or torn. It will be quite painful, harmful, and eventually fatal. At best it will leave a person handicapped. In the same way breaking the one-to-one bond of marriage will make the couple, in fact all of the immediate family, wounded—psychologically, physically, and socially. Among the worst consequences are sexually transmitted diseases, the deadly AIDS, and unwanted pregnancy.

8. The Scriptures prohibit not only adultery but also the very thought and desire of adultery (Matthew 5:27). Every evil deed is the result of premeditated thought (James 1:14-15). It is, therefore, extremely important for a person to control his or her thoughts or desires. It is only by self-control and by exercising our God-given sexuality in the right way, which is God's way, that we can live safely.

Sexuality and the EECMY

The Ethiopian Evangelical Church Mekane Yesus (EECMY) serves the whole person, caring for the physical as well as the spiritual needs of people. Human beings are a unity, made up of body, soul, and spirit (1 Thessalonians 5:23). It is this whole person that the church is called by God to serve.

The EECMY believes in Jesus Christ, who is her head and foundation (Ephesians 5:23; 1 Corinthians 3:11). In its constitution the EECMY declares that it accepts the word of the triune God, the three ecumenical creeds, the unaltered Augsburg confession, and Luther's catechisms as the basis of her faith. The work of the EECMY in relation to HIV/AIDS and sexually transmitted diseases (STDs) will be congruent with the biblical understanding of human sexuality described above and with the calling and confessional commitments of the church.

Why the EECMY Deals with HIV/AIDS

The word of God says, "How does God's love abide in anyone who has the world's goods and sees a brother or sister in need and yet refuses help? Little children, let us love, not in word or speech, but in truth and action" (1 John 3:16-18).

The basis of the EECMY concern for people in physical need is God's concern for his creation. Human beings, made by God, are a unity, comprised of body, soul, and spirit. God cares for every aspect of creation, giving rain and providing whatever is needed for human life here on earth. Jesus in his earthly ministry showed his care for people's physical as well as eternal needs. The church, following the Lord, cares for the well-being of people in all aspects, including their physical health. For this reason the EECMY, in cooperation with mission partners from abroad, is engaged in health services, education, and other development activities beneficial to the community. This includes creating awareness of HIV/AIDS so that people can protect themselves from the virus as well as care for people who are living with the disease, their orphans, and relatives.

On the Use of the Condom

For the EECMY, sex is something given by God to human beings that must be practiced in a responsible way. Our use of the gift of sexuality can be safe and bring us joy only when it is exercised in the right way, with one partner in a lasting one-to-one commitment. Whether one uses condoms or not, sexual intercourse outside of marriage is sinful before God. Even if a man who practices sexual intercourse outside of marriage manages to protect himself from sexually transmitted diseases through the use of a condom (though the protection is not 100% reliable), he has damaged his conscience and soul by being unfaithful to his partner (even risking her very life, should he contract the disease) and to God. Therefore our church does not accept any sex outside the marriage bond, with or without condom. Sex within a one-to-one lasting commitment is the only safe sex, both for the protection of the body as well as the psyche, which are united and influence one another.

The EECMY does not deny the externally protective role that condoms may play. However our church addresses the question of sexual faithfulness and sexual purity according to the Scriptures. That does not mean the church opposes a scientific discovery (such as the condom) that enhances or protects people's physical well-being. The church claims, however, to have a message from God that will keep those who receive it and live in it healthy and whole, physically as well as spiritually.

The church's concern is for the physical well-being as well as the spiritual well-being of people, and so it proclaims its message to that end. The church believes that the counsel of God, with which the church is entrusted, can work attitudinal change. This work is necessary, because, as long as people's attitudes and behaviors are not changed, condoms cannot give a secure and lasting solution to the risk of HIV/AIDS, neither in the life of an individual nor in the society.

The condom is like the fig leaves that Adam and Eve sewed to cover themselves when they found themselves naked after their disobedience (Genesis 3:7). They used their best wisdom to cover their nakedness. Their remedy was useful, but insufficient. Character and relational problems are best rectified by following the Creator God and his counsel. God made a lasting and enduring garment for them by shedding the blood of an animal (Genesis 3:21). Therefore, the EECMY promotes and teaches the lasting solution for the problem of AIDS and STD, which is the character change brought about by turning to the ways of the Creator. On the basis of the word of God, the church teaches the requirement of an absolute one-to-one sexual fidelity.

On Premarital Sex

As we have seen earlier, children are under the care of their parents until they reach the age of maturity. According to Scripture one can only engage in sexual intercourse after the age of maturity and only in a lifelong one-to-one relationship. Therefore the EECMY cannot approve premarital sex.

The advice given by the elderly Paul to the young Timothy indicates a scriptural perspective on Christian character and premarital sex. Timothy was advised, "Do not speak harshly to an older man, but speak to him as to a father, to younger men as brothers, to older women as mothers, to younger women as sisters—with absolute purity" (1 Timothy 5:1-2). Again, "Shun youthful passions and pursue righteousness, faith, love, and peace, along with those who call on the Lord from a pure heart" (2 Timothy 2:22). Therefore our church teaches young boys and girls to keep themselves sexually pure before marriage for their own benefit.

It should be stressed that keeping oneself sexually pure before marriage is a gain and not a loss. The law is given by God for one's advantage and not disadvantage in view of the psychological agony of broken relationships and the many sexually transmitted diseases, especially the deadly HIV/AIDS. God is not against our use or enjoyment of sex. However he wants all his people to use sex in a proper way, i.e., in a way that will not bring harm to them. Enjoyment is not enjoyment in the wrong context. It will be like a foolish man climbing up a falling tree near a lake to eat the honey hanging over the water. As he climbs up, the tree bends down into the lake because of the weight and the man loses his life, either by drowning or being eaten by crocodiles. He should have counted the cost of the honey. The consequences of premarital sex are similar. The remedy is the one-to-one lasting commitment of opposite sexes that is marriage.

On the One-to-One Relationship

The EECMY fully supports and teaches the one-to-one relationship that is supported by the Scriptures. The agreement to live in such a relationship should be made officially before God and his people. After the marriage vow is made before God and his people, it should be kept until death. This is the safest, surest, and God-approved way to keep individuals, families, and the community at large from HIV/AIDS and STDs. Such a family will produce healthy children who will then be good citizens when they grow.

Pastoral Care for People Living with HIV/AIDS and Their Families

In the exercise of pastoral care, the church takes the role of the good shepherd caring for the flock. The flock are people who are in any need of help, care, and attention, physically as well as psychologically. In the process of counseling it is important for the caregiver to listen to the patient and create an atmosphere where he or she can express himself or herself freely. Thus, it is very important to win the trust of the people whom we want to counsel—a process that will take time and patience.

AIDS is a disease for which no cure has been found. In Africa, AIDS is transmitted primarily through sexual intercourse with a person who is infected by the HIV virus. The pastor or counselor has to help the patient come to terms with having a terminal illness, understanding the patient's psychological, biological, and social needs.

People living with HIV/AIDS will often respond initially with disbelief, fear, and agitation. The counselor must provide practical and emotional support. Later, when the patient starts to adjust to the new situation, he or she might be filled with anger, depression, guilt, or anxiety. Sometimes he or she might withdraw from work, family, and home. At this point it is important to encourage the involvement of family and friends. Eventually, the patient can reach a stage of acceptance of the situation. Pastoral contacts should be strengthened and continued. Discussions from the Bible and prayers can be part of the care. The final stage, for people without life-prolonging medications, is preparation for death. Patients could have feelings of abandonment, isolation, and pain. It is important to talk to the patient and be alert to unfinished tasks and things they may need to make straight in their own lives and family.

The counselor should understand that from the view of God's forgiveness in the gospel, people living with HIV/AIDS are no different from any other person. In God's sight, all have sinned and fallen short of the glory of God, and all are in need of forgiveness. Some may have contracted the disease through their own sin or carelessness; others may have been innocent victims. The pastor will reach out to each appropriately in the name of Jesus. Our Lord Jesus Christ came to this world to help and save people exactly with such needs. "Those who are well have no need of a physician," he said, "but those who are sick. Go and learn what this means, 'desire mercy, not sacrifice,' for I have come to call not the righteous but sinners" (Matthew 9:12-13).

Therefore, whether HIV/AIDS has come into one's life by improper sexual relations or otherwise, it must be made clear that Jesus is very near to such people. The counselor can assure the patient and tell the truth of God's acceptance through Jesus Christ. In short, God loves the patient.

The second area of counseling is in regard to the necessary external precautions. First, of course, the person has to admit that he or she has the virus or the disease. Pre-test and post-test counseling can help towards this end. Once the diagnosis is accepted, the patient must learn the necessary precautions to avoid transmitting the disease to his or her sexual partner and other people.

The third area for counseling involves the immediate family and relatives of the patient. They need to know that the disease is not transmitted by normal contacts, but only through sexual contact or the exchange of blood. This kind of counseling needs to be extended to the neighborhood and the community at large.

The pastor can tell clients that they are in God's hand, that God knows their past, present, and future. The pastor can also tell them that they are the focus of God's love in Jesus Christ, regardless of past wrongs or past experiences of abuse and exploitation. The pastor can also encourage the client to accept the situation and trust in God.

Home-Based Care

Since sick people often stay with their families or relatives, it is important for us to know why and how we should care for the sick with us. We care for the sick, of course, because they are our relatives, because they are created in the image of God, and because God calls us to provide for those in need.

There are models already available of how to care for sick people without ourselves being infected. For example, a tuberculosis patient is cared for by isolating him or her and the utensils they use. A patient who is sick with jaundice is also cared for with good hygiene so that no transmission of the disease occurs. With simple precautions, HIV/AIDS is less contagious than many communicable diseases. Therefore, families, close relatives, and communities have no reason to panic.

Caring for the destitute, the poor, and the sick has been the primary way of expressing and living Christian love by Christian communities throughout the centuries. This extends not only to the care of the sick but also to the widows and orphans. "Religion that is pure and undefiled before God, the Father, is this: to care for orphans and widows in their distress, and to keep oneself unstained by the world" (James 1:27). Therefore, it is very important for all of us to care for orphans who have lost their parents because of HIV/AIDS by giving them shelter, food, clothing, and the necessities of life. Likewise, widows who have lost their husbands or men who have lost their wives should be comforted and helped in all their needs.

At home, people with HIV/AIDS should be treated like any other patient with a terminal illness, such as cancer. They should be approached in love and given all the services they need, while exercising proper care to avoid the kinds of contact that make possible the transmission of the HIV virus. Scripture praises those who care for the sick and the destitute. Our Lord speaks the final word when he says, "Then the king will say to those at his right hand, 'Come, you that are blessed by my Father, inherit the kingdom prepared for you from the foundation of the world; for I was hungry and you gave me food, I was thirsty and you gave me something to drink, I was a stranger and you welcomed me, I was naked and you gave me clothing, I was sick and you took care of me. . ." (Matthew 25:34-36).

The Battle for Justification by Faith in the African Context

Introduction

The doctrine of justification by faith alone has been expounded emphatically in the letters of the Apostle Paul, especially in his two apologetic and didactic letters, namely, Galatians and Romans (e.g., Galatians 2:15-16; Romans 3:28). Thus the doctrine goes back to Paul, i.e., the New Testament. It can even be traced back to the Old Testament, as seen in Abraham's being made righteous before God.

After lapses of centuries, the centrality of the biblical doctrine of justification by faith came back to light in the writing and preaching of the Reformation of the sixteenth century. The Reformation, especially in the person of Martin Luther, tried to straighten the wrong teaching and practice of the doctrine of justification in the Roman Catholic Church. Thus, the Augsburg Confession of 1530 speaks about its understanding of the doctrine of justification in the following way:

> It is also taught among us that we cannot obtain forgiveness of sin and righteousness before God by our own merits, works, or satisfactions, but that we receive forgiveness of sin and become righteous before God by grace, for Christ's sake, through faith, when we believe that Christ suffered for us and that

for his sake our sin is forgiven and righteousness and eternal life are given to us. For God will regard and reckon this faith as righteousness, as Paul says in Romans 3:21-26 and 4:5 (CA IV).[1]

The message of the Reformation brought forth the churches of the Reformation, which were later called Protestants by their opponents. After that, there was mutual doctrinal condemnation both in the Lutheran Confessions and by the Roman Catholic Church's Council of Trent. But for some time the Lutheran World Federation and the Pontifical Council for Promoting Christian Unity have been striving to understand each other's positions on the doctrine of justification and to seek common ground. As a result of this dialogue they have come up with a document entitled "Joint Declaration on the Doctrine of Justification" (Geneva, 1995). In light of this attempt to bring Lutherans and Romans Catholics together and to end the long-standing battle over the doctrine of justification by faith, I will now proceed to briefly survey the battle for justification by faith in the African context.

The Specific Ethiopian Context

Before surveying the broader African context, I would like to describe the specific Ethiopian situation with which I am familiar. The Christian church has existed in Ethiopia since the first half of the fourth century (330 A.D.). The church is presently called the Ethiopian Orthodox Church.

For years the Ethiopian Orthodox Church had a direct link with the Coptic Church of Egypt. It was only in the middle of this century that the church became autonomous.

From the beginning, the Protestants had to battle with the Ethiopian Orthodox Church over the doctrine of justification

---

1 Theodore G. Tappert, trans. and ed., *The Book of Concord* (Philadelphia: Fortress, 1959), 30.

by faith. The position of the Ethiopian Orthodox Church on the doctrine of justification can readily be seen from its traditional church-school curriculum. Any person who wants admission into the diaconate and priesthood has to learn the Ethiopie alphabet and the first seven verses of the First Epistle of St. John. After that, he has to read books such as a synoptic Gospel, the Tamira Maryam (the Miracles of Mary), the Gabata Hawaria (the Seven Epistles)—one of James, two of Peter, three of John, and one of Jude—the Psalter, and a portion of St. John's Gospel. When a candidate completes the above study he receives the diaconate from the bishop before marriage and later the priesthood after acquiring the technical knowledge of the services.[2]

From the traditional curriculum of the church outlined above we can see that Paul's epistles to the Galatians and the Romans (which are the central letters of St. Paul on the doctrine of justification by faith) are not included, at least on the level of education which leads to the diaconate and priesthood. On the contrary, the Epistle of James, which puts emphasis on faith and good works, is taken as part of the basic curriculum. One also may note that while Protestants see Jesus Christ as our only mediator and redeemer, the Ethiopian Orthodox Church adds saints, especially Mary, the mother of our Lord. These examples demonstrate that the Ethiopian Orthodox Church holds that faith and good works are needed for justification.

The first Protestant missionaries who came to Ethiopia did not come to start a new church but to reform the already existing Orthodox Church. However, as in Europe so also in Ethiopia did the reformers meet opposition and persecution. Nevertheless, they gained some adherents among the Orthodox priests who understood their message, and the battle for the doctrine of

---

2 Aymro Wondmagegnhu and Joachim Motovu, *The Ethiopian Orthodox Church* (Addis Ababa: Berhanena Selam, 1970), 38.

justification by faith continued. The end result was the formation of the Protestant churches of Ethiopia.

Among many reformers in the Orthodox Church, one may cite Ato Meseret Sibhat Leab, Aleqa Taye, Qes Badima Yalew, and Ato Gorfu Abreha.

In his famous doctrinal book called *Sima Tsdq Beherawi*, Ato Meseret writes:

> While righteousness is one, there are two ways to achieve it. The first one is that which a man ought to get by works. The second is the one given by the covenant of grace which man receives only by faith. The first righteousness, revealed in the Law, is the one which leads to the righteousness to be received by faith alone given by the free grace of God, and it cannot justify man. . . . The righteousness of the Law requires that man be found blameless from the very beginning. The gift of righteousness from God, however, makes a sinner righteous by grace without any good deeds because of faith in Jesus Christ and his blood, whom God made the atoning sacrifice. As there is no one without sin except Jesus Christ, who was blameless and fulfilled the demands of the Law, man can only be righteous at the moment when he receives the merits of Christ on account of the righteousness given by grace of God alone. This righteousness is the foundation for holy life and creates the desire for a holy life. Therefore we confess that righteousness reveals the free state of man before God's justice and that it cannot be earned as a wage. . . . Therefore, we oppose those who think that righteousness can be found in any other way

and those who say "let us sin that grace and righteousness may abound."³

Ato Meseret Sibhat Leab is still an Orthodox Christian. However, due to his view on justification by faith alone, he was thrown out of the Orthodox Theological College.

One other point which is directly related to the doctrine of justification by faith is the place given to Jesus Christ in the art, music, and liturgy of the church in Ethiopia. In the Orthodox Church there are many icons of angels (such as Gabriel, Michael, Urael, and Rafael) and saints (such as St. Tekle Haimanot, St. Paul, and St. Mary) who are invoked for the forgiveness of sin and restoration of physical and spiritual health. In the Protestant churches, where justification by faith alone is taught, Jesus Christ is the center of worship. The liturgies of the Protestant churches convey the same idea. In the Ethiopian Orthodox Church, however, it is taught that man can be saved by faith and good works; the angels and saints stand side by side with Jesus Christ in Orthodox art, liturgy, and music.

Ato Gorfu Aberha, a reformer in the Orthodox Church, writes in his book about the complete sufficiency of the work of God through Christ on the cross for justification. He uses an enlightening local illustration of a clay pot. According to his illustration, if a clay pot is broken the gathering of a thousand clay pots cannot restore it back to normal. Likewise, the brokenness that fell upon Adam (humankind) because of sin cannot be restored by any other creature except the Creator Jesus Christ, the Son of God, who is the radiance of God's glory and the exact representation of his being (Hebrews 1:3). By this illustration, Ato Gorfu Aberha opposes the longstanding and common belief

---

3 Translated from the Amharic: *Meseret Sibhat Leab, Sima Tsdq Beherawi* (Addis Ababa: Artistic, 1958), 93-94.

in the Orthodox Church that the saints play a role in restoring one's relationship with God.[4]

Evangelicals in general agree with the Orthodox reformers mentioned above. As a result many evangelicals have had to face persecution or imprisonment either for their teaching of justification by faith alone or for teaching the all sufficiency of Jesus Christ in the redemptive act.

The Battle for Justification by Faith within Protestantism

We all know that the doctrine of justification by faith alone is the cardinal doctrine among Protestants. As Luther says, it is "the master and prince, the lord, the ruler, and the judge over all kinds of doctrines; it preserves and governs all church doctrine and raises up our conscience before God. Without this article the world is utter death and darkness."[5] Nevertheless, some Protestants themselves have problems when it comes to the practice of justification by faith in the Ethiopian context. As a result they require that people perform certain rituals or have a visible experience to confirm the authenticity of their faith. This has created a battle for the doctrine of justification by faith alone in the context of African Protestantism, and especially in Ethiopia.

Among Ethiopian Protestants one of the crucial matters related to the doctrine of justification by faith alone is the mode of Baptism. A Christian who has been baptized as an infant is considered not to have received a valid Baptism, which is defined as adult Baptism in deep waters. This has created a lot of tension between the Ethiopian Evangelical Church Mekane Yesus (a Lutheran church administering infant Baptism and accepting those from the Orthodox Church without rebaptism) and other

---
4 Yemenfes Qidus Abraha, *Tegsatsna Mikir* (Addis Ababa: St. George, 1967), 86-93.
5 Ewald Plass, *What Luther Says* (St. Louis: Concordia, 1959), 2: 703.

Protestants such as Baptists and Pentecostals, who insist upon rebaptizing anyone who has been baptized as an infant before taking them into their membership. In addition, they consider those who are baptized as infants as "second class Christians," while they constitute the "first grade Christians" who have received adult Baptism by immersion. Here we find a battle for justification by faith alone. Are we justified by faith alone in Jesus Christ or by the mode of Baptism we administer? Is the right mode of Baptism an additional requirement for justification? We believe that there is one Baptism. A particular mode of Baptism such as immersion cannot be taken as a must for all Christians for salvation. To do that is to demand an additional work besides justification by faith alone.

John R. W. Stott makes the point clear by applying Galatians 2:11-16, where St. Paul comments on St. Peter's refusal to eat with the Gentile Christians when the Judaizers from Jerusalem come. He writes:

> Still today various Christian bodies and people repeat Peter's mistake. They refuse to have fellowship with professing Christian believers unless they have been totally immersed in water (no other form of baptism will satisfy them), or unless they have been episcopally confirmed (they insist that only the hands of a bishop in the historic succession will do), or unless their skin has a particular color, or unless they come out of a certain social drawer (usually the top one), and so on. All this is a grievous affront to the gospel. Justification is by faith alone; we have no right to add a particular mode of baptism or confirmation or any denominational, racial or social conditions. God does not insist on these things before he accepts us into fellowship; so we must not

insist upon them either. What is this ecclesiastical exclusiveness which we practice and which God does not? Are we more stand-offish than he? The only barrier to communion with God, and therefore with each other, is unbelief, a lack of saving faith in Jesus Christ.[6]

While the Baptists like to add the right mode of Baptism to the doctrine of justification by faith alone, the Pentecostals add a special spiritual experience. For example, Pentecostals insist that Christians, if genuine, will speak in tongues and enjoy other more miraculous spiritual gifts.

The topic of Christian freedom also comes into question in connection with issues considered to be adiaphora. Can a Christian use alcohol moderately and with self-control? Can a Christian smoke? How should the church treat culturally accepted polygamous marriages contracted before one became a Christian? There are some who teach that any use of alcohol, moderate or excessive, is sin. For some, even to use alcoholic wine in Holy Communion is considered to be sin. How do such things relate to the doctrine of justification by faith alone?

Our church wants to stress Christian freedom and the idea that a man is not justified by what he does or does not do but by faith in Jesus Christ alone. At the same time, our church teaches that anything in excess which is without self-control and moderation is sinful. The battle for justification by faith alone rages on similar grounds between the Protestant denominations in Africa. In one form or another "works righteousness" is injected (in the name of *exceeding* spirituality) instead of justification by faith alone.

---

6 John R. W. Stott, *Only One Way: The Message of Galatians* (Downers Grove, Illinois: InterVarsity Press, 1968), 5-7.

The Battle for Justification by Faith within a Denomination

The doctrine of justification by faith is more often correctly stated rather than practiced. Within a number of Protestant denominations, although the doctrine is expressly stated, there is discrepancy in practice. For example, a number of Protestant denominations tell their members to tithe and give offerings so that they may get an equivalent reward from God. The idea of giving out of free will with joy is not stressed. Rather, offering is made as a work to be accomplished to get the favor of God.

The Ethiopian Evangelical Church Mekane Yesus has as her basis of faith the Holy Scriptures of the Old and New Testaments, the creeds of the ancient church, the Augsburg Confession, and Luther's catechisms. Because of this, we can say that the church follows the theology of the Reformation when it comes to the doctrine of justification by faith. In addition to her confessional documents, the Lutheran liturgy (which is used in all her congregations) plays an important role in promoting the doctrine of justification by faith alone. The Mekane Yesus Church and a smaller sister Lutheran Church in Ethiopia are the only Protestant churches using a written liturgy in a proper way. Furthermore, the official hymnal used by the church demonstrates her faith in the doctrine of justification by faith alone. Great care is taken when incorporating new songs into the church's hymnal so that the theology conforms to the doctrine of justification by faith.

In his book *The Word of God in Ethiopian Tongues*, Eskil Forslund has studied 196 selected sermons from the Ethiopian Evangelical Church Mekane Yesus. His study shows that the sermons teach justification by faith alone. However, salvation in the context of these sermons does not mean forgiveness of sin alone. It is much more than that. It includes physical well-being as well as victory over evil powers. During the times of persecution by the Communists or other local people, sermons emphasize God's surpassing and protective power. Forslund writes:

> The preachers affirm that no human being can obtain salvation through his own efforts. Salvation is God's gift to mankind for the sake of Jesus Christ. However, the preachers point out man's role and action when salvation is offered to him by God: all categories of preachers underscore the importance of making a decision to have a personal relationship with Christ. A Christian is one who has received or accepted Christ. This feature is found in the sermons of all seasons of the church year. . . . All categories of preachers deal with the theme of salvation from the aspects of forgiveness of sin, healing, and powerful acts of God against evil forces. *These themes* occur side by side in the sermon material. It is, however, possible to discern a tendency in the sermons of more recent years in which the preachers emphasized God's power and protection when people resist or harass the Church: "God fought for his people" and "The Lord is a man of war" are expressions and biblical quotations representative for this later period. Sermons from earlier years tend to emphasize God's power in resisting evil spiritual powers: Jesus has authority not only over evil spirits . . . but over the whole life of man. The different aspects of salvation in the sermon material do not appear as opposing views on this topic, nor does any single aspect dominate over the other, even though the aspect of forgiveness is very strong. The different aspects are rather attempts to interpret salvation

as delivery and freedom from various negative and threatening dimensions of human life.[7]

In spite of the above understanding, the danger of confusing justification and sanctification has always been there. There is pressure to see a certain kind of demonstrable good deed (a sign), either physical or spiritual, if a person claims to have been justified. An improper emphasis on good deeds without prior acknowledgment of the foundation, which is justification by faith alone, will be misleading.

The Doctrine of Justification in the Broader African Context

For Manas Buthelezi of South Africa, salvation is not only being made righteous before God from personal sin but also being whole in all aspects of life. Righteousness should lead a person to have a better understanding of himself, as God intended him to have. Any sociological, economic, or political arrangement that does not promote or respect man's right to be his own self is dehumanizing. For Buthelezi, since redemption does not mean the absolute abolition of the trace of sin in man, the creation of the new man in Christ does not mean the substitution but the restoration of the old. Buthelezi writes:

> The passport to the place of receiving God's gifts is opportunity in education, employment, and general development. To deny a person these opportunities is to displace him from his God-given place; it is to alienate him from the wholeness of life.[8]

For South African theologians, justification by faith does not remain in the realm of the soul but should encompass the social, economic, and political realms, so that man may be whole.

---

[7] Eskil Forslund, *The Word of God in Ethiopian Tongues* (Uppsala: Swedish Institute for Missionary Research, 1993), 142-145.

[8] John Parratt, *A Reader in African Christian Theology* (London: SPCK, 1987), 100.

We can also assess the doctrine of justification by faith from the perspective of religion. Dr. Richard J. Gehman, who has made a thorough study of African traditional religion, writes the following:

> The African Traditional Religion (ATR) does not teach that sin is rebellion against God or transgression of God's law. Instead, the traditional way of life is the best life which has been given by the ancestral spirits, the divinities and by God himself. There is no understanding of a spiritual new birth, a need to grow and progress in the knowledge of God. Since the status quo is the best, man's primary concern is material prosperity and prestige. . . . In ATR the stress is upon a good life here and now. But the Christian faith focuses on the past, present and future aspects of our salvation. . . . This salvation is by grace through faith alone. All other religions, including some Christian churches, emphasize human effort, good works, personal merit, keeping the commandments, obeying God and controlling the flesh in order to merit salvation. ATR is no exception.[9]

While remarking on the concept of sin as an antisocial act, Tokunboh Adeyemo writes the following:

> If an antisocial act is all there is to sin, salvation from sin would be in the same terms. Thus, it is plain in the oral traditions that to be saved primarily means to be accepted. One is first accepted to the community of the living by being good to one's neighbors, and secondly accepted among the com-

---

9 Richard J. Gehman, *African Traditional Religion* (Kijabe, Kenya: East African Educational Publishers, Ltd., 1989), 254.

munity of the dead ancestors by remembering them through libations, prayers and offerings. An aspect of this acceptance is the struggle for power or "vital force." It is believed that one who excels his equals has been specially favored by the ancestors and that such an honor is indicative of salvation.[10]

How do we evaluate the above understanding of salvation in the African traditional religion? The best way is to evaluate it in the light of what the Scriptures teach. The Scriptures clearly teach justification by faith alone; anyone who teaches a doctrine which differs from it is declared to be anathema. In our doctrine of justification Christ is central. It is by grace alone and by faith in Christ alone that we are justified. This, however, does not mean that the spiritual and physical blessings that follow one's faith in Christ do not show their imprint on social human conditions. It has been repeatedly reported that true faith in Jesus Christ has a positive effect on an individual's and a community's well-being.

Joint Declaration on the Doctrine of Justification

As has been stated earlier, the Lutheran World Federation and the Pontifical Council for Promoting Christian Unity have been in dialogue for more than twenty-five years concerning the doctrine of justification by faith alone. The consensus reached has been published under the title "Joint Declaration on the Doctrine of Justification" (Geneva, 1995).

From what is presented in the document as the "common understanding of justification" one can see that the two groups have tried their best to make themselves clear and find a common ground. On some points consensus or agreement seems possible. In many ways, the two views even seem to strengthen or com-

---

10 Tokunboh Adeyemo, *Salvation in African Tradition* (Nairobi: Evangel Publishing House, 1979), 93.

plement each other. For example, in the section "Justification as Forgiving Sins and Making Righteous," it is stated:

> When Lutherans understand the grace of God above all as forgiving love, they do not thereby deny the life-renewing power of grace. Rather their intention is to insist that God's gracious action remains free from human conditions and is not dependent on the life-renewing effects of grace in human beings.
>
> On the other hand, "When Catholics emphasize the life-renewing effects of grace in believers, they do not deny that God's gracious action remains free from human conditions. Rather it is their intention to insist that the forgiving grace of God always imparts a gift of active love in the Holy Spirit."[11]

When one reads such statements from both sides, one can see that the two views complement and support each other. Nevertheless, there are areas in which agreement or consensus is still distant. For example, the formulation on the good works of the justified is stated in nearly the traditional manner. The statement says that ". . . when Catholics affirm the meritorious character of good works their intention is to emphasize human responsibility. By so doing they do not intend to contest the character of those works as gifts, or far less to deny that justification always remains the unmerited gift of grace." On the other hand, "Lutherans understand good works, the fruits and signs of justification, in the sense of the New Testament concept of reward, that is, as gratuitous gift and not as merit.

In my view the above two positions are incompatible. We believe that Christians have responsibility to live a life worthy of their calling. This has been stated repeatedly in the Scriptures.

---

11 *Joint Declaration on the Doctrine of Justification* (Geneva, 1995), 6.

However, it is something else to say these good deeds have a meritorious character. If justification is by faith alone or if it is an unmerited gift of grace, that should be stated in a clear manner and in unequivocal language.

Conclusion

The battle for the doctrine of justification by faith alone rages everywhere. It rages within churches, within denominations, and even within individuals. Justification by faith is a gift from God. It is receiving the finished work of Christ. Justification by faith is the working of the Holy Spirit. Human beings in their societies and religions tend to give themselves credit for their work and religiosity. But the Apostle Paul says such desire is the work of the flesh. No one can be reconciled with God by his good deeds, as we learn from Galatians 3:2-5.

We need also to remember the poignant statements of Martin Luther on this important article of faith:

> The doctrine of justification must . . . be diligently learned; for in it all the articles of our faith are comprehended. And when that is safe, the others are safe too. This doctrine is the head and the cornerstone. It alone begets, nourishes, builds, preserves, and defends the church of God; and without it the church of God cannot exist for one hour. . . . For no one who does not hold this article or, to use Paul's expression, this "sound doctrine" (Titus 2:1) is able to teach aright in the church or successfully to resist any adversary. . . . This is the heel of the Seed that opposes the old serpent and crushes its head. That is why Satan, in turn, cannot but persecute it.[12]

---

12 Plass, 703-704

Therefore, justification by faith alone for Christ's sake is the only consolation we have as Christians. As all planes going up from the ground finally come down and land, any human attempt to please God should come down and rest in the Son of God, our Lord Jesus Christ, about whom God said, "This is my Son, whom I love; with him I am well pleased" (Matthew 3:16).

The Theology of the Cross in the African Context

Introduction

Africa has always been related to the cross ever since the Suffering Servant, our Lord Jesus Christ, found himself heading to Golgotha, carrying the cross. Simon, the father of Alexander and Rufus, who helped our Lord carry the cross, was from Cyrene, an important Libyan city in North Africa.[1] After the resurrection, the Ethiopian eunuch was among the first to hear the message of the cross from Philip the Evangelist as the two traveled to Gaza. The eunuch was reading the text of the Suffering Servant from Isaiah 53. Still today, Africa is close to the cross of Christ in many respects. The focus of this essay is to show the multi-dimensional relevance of Christ's cross within the African experience and reality.

Historical Background: The Cross as a Way of Capital Punishment

The Roman Empire most likely inherited the cross as an instrument of capital punishment from the Carthaginians.[2] This cruel instrument of punishment was used in the empire partic-

---
1 William Barclay, *The Gospel of Mark* (Edinburgh: St. Andrew, 1975), 360. CF. also the study note on Mark 15:21 in *The New International Version Study Bible* (Grand Rapids: Zondervan, 1995), 1526.
2 "Cross," *The New International Dictionary of New Testament Theology*, ed. Colin Brown (Grand Rapids: Zondervan, 1975), 1:392.

ularly against rebellious foreigners, violentnt criminals, robbers, and slaves.[3] It was a horrible punishment. Death on the cross was slow. Besides the hunger, scourging, and the ill treatment endured by the victim, he also had to carry the horizontal bar of the cross to the place of the crucifixion. There, after lying on the ground, the hands of the criminal were nailed or tied with a rope to the bar. After that the criminal was hung on the vertical bar that had been erected on the site of the crucifixion. The crucified person then had to suffer from the heat and cold, the bites of insects and birds, as well as complete exhaustion. One of the victim's great problems was the inability to breathe as the weight of his body pulled him down. After this prolonged, excruciating suffering, the criminal died. Sometimes the victim's bones were broken so he would not be able to support his body, which would hasten his inability to breathe, thus hastening death. Seneca, the Roman writer, observes the following concerning the awfulness of death on the cross:

> Can anyone be found who would prefer wasting away in pain dying limb by limb, or letting out his life drop by drop, rather than expiring once for all? Can any man be found willing to be fastened to the accursed tree, long sickly, already deformed, swelling with ugly weals on shoulders and chest, and drawing the breath of life amid long-drawn-out agony? He would have many excuses for dying even before mounting the cross.[4]

As to the shape of the cross, two kinds are suggested. The one looks like the English letter T, while the other variety looks like the plus sign (+). Because of the inscription over the head,

---

[3] Martin Hengel, *Crucifixion in the Ancient World and the Folly of the Message of the Cross* (Philadelhia: Fortress, 1977).

[4] Hengel, *Crucifixion*, 30-31.

many think the kind of cross upon which our Lord was crucified might have had the shape of the plus sign.[5]

What is important theologically is not to master the details of death on the cross, however beneficial they may be as historical description. The important thing is to know that the cross is the greatest suffering a person may experience. Why did the innocent Son of God die on the cross? What does Jesus' suffering and death mean within our African experience? We must consider our Lord's death in light of the African personal, social, political, and economic life. These are some of the areas we will address.

The African and the Shedding of Blood

The author of the book of Hebrews opens for us a door to find God in light of Christ's cross:

> Therefore, brothers, since we have confidence to enter the Most Holy Place by the blood of Jesus, by a new and living way opened for us through the curtain, that is, his body, and since we have a great priest over the house of God, let us draw near to God with a sincere heart in full assurance of faith, having our hearts sprinkled to cleanse us from a guilty conscience and having our bodies washed with pure water (Hebrews 10:19-22).

Africans, like most people in the world, are highly religious. In fact, their worldview and daily existence are permeated by their religious convictions and practices. Whether they farm, trade, or select a bride for their children, their daily living is full of religious meaning. Besides religious practices connected with daily vocations, Africans want to reach the divine and please him. For that purpose they may sometimes use intermediaries such

---

[5] Tokunboh Adeyemo, *Salvation in African Tradition* (Nairobi: Evangel, 1997), 33-35.

as rainmakers, ritual elders, diviners, medicine men, etc. These intermediaries prescribe to them certain things to be performed. One of the most prominent prescribed rituals is sacrifice.

The practice and concept of shedding blood for religious purpose is not new for Africans. The sacrifice, especially of animals, has been widely used. The animal sacrificed could be a chicken, a lamb, a goat, or an ox. Sometimes a specific color is prescribed. Why do Africans in general like to sacrifice? It is because of their respect for the divine. It is to be on good terms with the powers that have authority in their daily lives. Their aim is to be obedient so they may be successful in life and also may be saved from the different misfortunes that may occur.[6] Concerning sacrifice by Africans, John S. Mbiti writes:

> In African societies, life is closely associated with blood. When blood is shed in making a sacrifice, it means that human or animal life is being given back to God, who is in fact the ultimate source of all life. Therefore the purpose of such a sacrifice must be a very serious one. Such sacrifices may be made when the lives of many people are in danger. The life of one person or animal, or of a few of either, is destroyed in the belief that this will save the life of many people. Thus, the destruction of one becomes the protection of many.[7]

The death of an animal and the shedding of its blood speak loudly to the religious aspirations of the African continent. Otherwise nobody would go to the pain of finding an animal that will

---

[6] The Oromos of the Adama Bosset area sacrifice to appease and pray to *Wakayo*, their god. After the animal is killed, its blood is sprinkled on the trunk of the tree, the green grass, and the people. Some of the meat is roasted to be eaten by the people after a little is burned as a sacrifice to *Wakayo*. Cf. Girmay Tekle, "Socio-Cultural Analysis of Adama Bosset District" (unpublished paper, July 2000).

[7] John S. Mbiti, *Introduction to African Religion*, 2nd ed. (Nairobi: East African Educational Publishers, 1991), 63.

cost him money and take time to raise. There is an inherent sensitivity in the African to the need for some kind of substitutionary sacrifice to approach and please the divine.

From this point of view, the death of Christ on the cross as the substitution for the sinner is a welcome message for the African people. It is not something new or strange to the African culture, but it makes perfect what has been imperfect. In the African rituals of animal sacrifice, we can find some congruence with the Jewish practice of sacrifice. Just as the Jewish sacrifices prepared them for the ultimate and perfect sacrifice effected on the cross, the African religious culture of sacrifice prepared the mind and hearts of the people for the perfect sacrifice on the cross. Therefore, a believing African can identify himself or herself without any problem with the words of St. Peter: "For you know that it was not with perishable things such as silver or gold that you were redeemed from the empty way of life handed down to you from your forefathers, but with the precious blood of Christ, a lamb without blemish or defect" (1 Peter 1:18-19).

As the result of Christ's death on the cross, the African people have found the way of salvation. It is through the cross of Christ that the African has received the privilege to approach God in a clear conscience without any remorse or guilt. The cross of Christ has opened for the Afrrican the way to heaven. All Africans who believe in the Lord Jesus Christ know that the way to heaven is wide open for them because of the cross of Christ, regardless of their external circumstances. In his suffering on the cross, Christ brought freedom and relief for the African conscience and mind.

The Cross of Christ as the Way of Victory

For Africans, there is no dichotomy between the world of the spirits and the physical world.[8] The two worlds are interde-

---

8 John Parratt, ed., *A Reader in African Christian Theology* (London: SPCK, 1987), 87.

pendent and, so to speak, operate together. The nature spirits and different kinds of powers operate in their farm, health, birth, cattle, season, etc. Africans call upon the respective spirit to have the right relationship and favor. For example, the Wollaytta in southern Ethiopia considered the first week of the new moon holy. They did not cultivate the fields on the Wednesdays of the first week of the new moon.[9] During this appointed holy day, they also approached the rainmakers and diviners so the gods would provide the necessary rain and health to tend the fields. Now, however, the Wollaytta have found Christ, the most powerful one. Many Africans now believe that Christ crucified and risen is greater than any power or spirit that has had authority over them. Therefore, through their faith in Christ, they are free from the fear of spirits, powers, and principalities.

The confrontation of principalities and powers has been a real phenomenon in the African churches. Whenever the African churches advanced with the message of Christ crucified, this confrontation of principalities and powers has occurred. Sometimes the evil spirits give way to the Spirit of Christ; at other times those who are opposed to the message of the cross resort to violent means.

The Cross as Suffering and Persecution Because of One's Faith

Some may think suffering and persecution because of one's confession of Christ is a relic of past history. However, in the experience of most African Christians it has been a vivid and recent experience. It will be wrong to assume that persecution will stop even in the future as long as there are different and opposing powers behind what the Apostle Paul calls "the flesh" and "the

---

9 Tetemke Yohanise Shonde, The *World View of Wolaita and Attempts to Contextualize the Gospel* (2000), 48.

Spirit." Of course the persecution may take different forms, from verbal attack to open violence, depending on the situation.

Believing individuals have been martyred for the faith and confession of the Lord Jesus Christ as Savior. The Ugandan martyrs and the female Ethiopian martyrs are good examples. Some have been tortured and imprisoned for years for their confession. A lot has yet to be written about the African confession of Christ and the suffering endured by believers on account of this living witness to the cross.[10]

The Sociopolitical Dimension of the Cross

The sociopolitical application of Christ's cross looks beyond what is normally known as the substitutionary death of Christ for our sins. It sees the opposition against human suffering, social injustice, and oppression and the subsequent price one may pay by opposing such systems as constituting the cross. Peter Kanyandago of Uganda writes: "The suffering of Jesus is not just a result of a free decision to deliver himself for our sins, but is a result of his stand against and opposition to religious and civil authorities who perpetuate the suffering of others."[11] While explaining his understanding of the cross and suffering. Kanyandago clarifies further the place and function of suffering under the cross.

---

10 An Ethiopian woman who was eight months pregnant was martyred by fanatic local people who belonged to the traditional Ethiopian Orthodox Church when she confessed Jesus Christ and became an evangelical Christian. This occurred in Amoute in the Gurage region. Cf. Shiferawu Zeleke, "The Martyrs of Amoute" (Bachelor of Theology paper, Mekane Yesus Seminary, Ethiopia). The gifted Ethiopian solo singer Tesfaye Gabiso and his friends were imprisoned for seven years in the Yirgalem Prison in southern Ethiopia because they confessed that "Jesus is Lord." These events took place under the Communist regime in Ethiopia during 1974-1991.

11 Hannah W. Kinoti and John M. Waliggo, eds., *The Bible in African Christianity* (Nairobi: Acton, 1997), 124.

Firstly, suffering does not come from God and is an inhuman experience that cannot be justified in any way without taking into account how it comes about. Secondly, a Christian's response, like that of Christ, must be to fight against it. Any type of theology, spirituality, or devotion that integrates and exalts suffering must be rejected. Thirdly, in the process of fighting against what causes suffering, one is bound to meet with opposition which can lead to suffering. This is the type of suffering that the cross represents and it can be accepted because it liberates others and leads to life.[12]

This idea of the cross, which has the backing of many African theologians and intellectuals, is similar to that of Professor Jon Sobrino of El Salvador. Professor Sobrino is against a purely academic theology, which fails to take an appropriate action in the practical life of people. He also is against the traditional mournful "mystique" of the cross, which is too passive and individualistic. For the cross to be relevant, it has to relate to the modern world and its social injustice. According to Sobrino, "God is to be found on the crosses of the oppressed."[13]

We have to appreciate the above views because they direct us to a holistic meaning and application of the cross of Christ. If we rightly understand and apply the cross of Christ, it is where differences are overcome and all become one. The best model and witness to the effects of the cross of Christ on human communities is the celebration of the eucharist. It is during this gathering for the partaking of Holy Communion where the body and blood of our Lord Jesus Christ is shared. The Apostle Paul clearly ad-

---

12 Kinoti and Waliggo, *Bible in African Christianity*, 124.
13 Jon Sobrino, *Christology at the Crossorads* (Maryknoll: Orbis, 1978), 201.

monishes that there should not be divisions because of social and economic standards among those who receive the eucharist. The poor who do not have any possessions are equal to the rich when they come to the table of the Lord. In fact, the agape meal that they share together after Holy Communion should be equally distributed, regardless of social status (1 Conrinthians 11:20-22, 33). The apostles repeatedly reiterate the equality of the people of God in the eucharistic celebration, in worship, and in daily living. This was indeed the practice of the early church (Acts 2:44-45). St. Luke reports in the Acts of the Apostles how: "All the believers where one in heart and mind. No one claimed that any of his possessions was his own, but they shared everything they had" (Acts 4:32). The apostles' teaching was that from where there is much blessing and abundance, it should be shared where there is a need so all shall be even or equal.

From the witness of the apostles, we can understand that the cross of Christ is the place where barriers of all kinds are erased as we share in the eucharist. The ethnic, economic, sexual, social, racial, and any other kind of barrier must disappear at the Lord's Table. This is the kind of community that our Lord Jesus Christ wanted to create through his death on the cross. This community, diverse yet united through the cross of Christ, can bring change in the society in which we live. Too often, however, the church, which is the community of the cross of Christ, has itself become a poor model instead of the light and the salt of the earth (Matthew 5:13).

Instead of "lifting high the cross" so the world may see it, the church has kept it within its premises. Only those who are permitted to go inside the church's walls have the opportunity to hear the Gospel's message. However, the vast majority of people live outside the church's premises and the gates of the city. While they know the cross as an emblem, they know little about its message and meaning. The Good News of the cross of Christ was not given only to those in the church. In fact, the original command of our Lord Jesus Christ says, "Go and make disciples of all nations" (Matthew 28:19).

The cross of Christ is not only the place of forgiveness, but it also is the place for justice. God showed both his perfect justice and his love on the cross. This means both the justice and love of God on the cross should find access into our human societies. In fact, the voices of Kanyandago and Sobrino are reactions against the silence and the impotency of the Christian churches to give a satisfactory meaning to a world full of suffering, social injustice, and poverty.

One of the most succinct definitions given about a human being is "body-soul-in community." If a human being is a "body-soul-in community," the cross of Christ has validity to everyone. As often indicated, the strict dichotomizing of the human being into two compartments, namely the body and soul, was a Greek idea and not a Hebrew idea. According to the biblical understanding, a human being is a unity. There is no division between the soul of a person and the body. The soul is the summing up of the whole personality.[14] In the twenty-first century we have come to understand in light of the biblical witness and our African context that a human being is not only the unity of body and soul. The body and soul do not exist in a vacuum. The person has a community that influences the body and soul. Therefore, a human being will fall short of being seen in totality unless the social system or community in which the individual lives is taken into consideration. Therefore, the cross of Christ, where the justice and love of God has been portrayed, should address all these aspects, including the social system.

---

14 "Soul," *Dictionary of New Testament Theology*, 3:680.

The Personal Element

The reality of the atonement through which the personal reconciliation with God is effected becaue of the cross of Christ should not be underestimated by any means. The New Testament points to many living examples of times our Lord Jesus Christ and the apostles preached to individuals and led them to faith. The story of Philip the Evangelist and the Ethiopian eunuch mentioned in Acts 8 is only one example. The Ethiopian, the first African official to encounter the message of the cross, was reading from the song of the Suffering Servant, which is recorded in Isaiah 53.

> He was led like a lamb to the slaughter, and as a sheep before her shearers is silent, so he did not open his mouth. By oppression and judgment he was taken away. And who can speak of his descendants? For he was cut off from the land of the living (Isaiah 53:7-8).

As can be seen from the text, the message explained to the Ethiopian was the good news about Jesus, which was the message of the cross. As an expression of his acceptance of the message, the Ethiopian asked Philip to baptize him (Cf. also Acts 2:38; Acts 17:30-34). For the Apostle Paul, the message of the cross was his all in all. The cross was the summary of his witness of the Gospel. He knew nothing but Christ crucified. The message of the cross was his norm and yardstick, not only to measure the teachings of others, but also as the most important signpost for his own teaching. The message of the cross was not something that Paul ingeniously devised, but it was revealed to him from God (Galatians 1:12). The cross is foolishness and a scandal to the world, but it is the power of God and the wisdom of God for those who are being saved.

The Christian's spiritual experiences, justification, peace, spiritual gifts, sanctification, and empowerment are the results of the cross. Christians live by identifying themselves with the death of Christ. Christians have died to the Law and sin when, through the sacrament of Holy Baptism, they have died and been buried with Christ to join in his resurrection to new life. In the gift of Baptism, Christians live a life of faith grounded in the power of the death and resurrection of Jesus. Christians now live by faith the life of the resurrection as if in this very moment they rose from the waters of Baptism. If we believe that societies and communities have to be governed in justice, it is important to have individuals who are reconciled with the God of justice who revealed himself in and through the cross. Knowing him will give such leaders the sense and meaning of divine justice, which is justice par excellence.

This is important because, as our Lord said, it is difficult to reap justice from someone who has no sense of justice. If individuals are the cornerstones of communities and societies, those individuals who are equipped with God's justice will make a tremendous contribution to their constituencies. God's perfect justice is best understood and appropriated under the sacrifice of his Son on the cross. The cross, therefore, provides a powerful global witness and signpost to affirm God's justice in the world.

Caring for Those in Physical Need

The cross of Christ is the greatest and highest expression of love for sinful humanity. Our Lord Jesus Christ alluded to his self-giving love on the cross when he said, "Greater love has no one than this, that he lay down his life for his friends" (John 15:13). However, making oneself accessible to others and caring for others starts by attending to their needs. There seem to be different levels of suffering or crosses one can take on in our world communities. The greatest is self-giving. Our Lord Jesus

Christ in the Gospels identified himself with the sick, the poor, the disadvantaged, and the socially neglected. He fed the hungry and healed the blind, the lepers, and those suffering from various ailments. He accepted the socially ostracized groups, such as Zacchaeus and Matthew, the tax collectors; the sinful woman who washed his feet with her tears; and the Samaritan woman at the well. Jesus wept with those who wept, as can be seen from the narrative concerning the death of Lazarus (John 11:33-35). In short, Jesus carried the infirmities of all.

We in Africa want to live this kind of identification and witness. We know about preaching. We have heard verbal preaching many times. What we want and look for are those who are like Jesus Christ; those who are willing to identify and care for the sick, the poor, and the disadvantaged; those who are willing to bring about change. Jesus did not stay in an ivory tower or his "pastor's office" to prepare his homily for the coming Sabbath. Although I am not against this kind of preparation, it is important to stress that Christ went to the suffering people and participated in alleviating their problems. Such identification is a way to carry the cross. This is among the first levels of self-giving, and it reaches its climax when one lays down one's life for the helpless and the disadvantaged. We expect all missionaries and evangelists to do this, but it is what is lacking in most missionary and evangelistic enterprises. Today, becoming a missionary is like going to a picnic. The missionary comes from his home country not to identify but to be highly paid in hard currency so he may have an easy life in the field in which he works. In our African context we find that an ivory tower called the "mission compound" is built so the missionary can live a peaceful and undisturbed life away from the crowds and the disadvantaged.

We, as African intellectuals, are not doing any better. Although we have better access and possibilities to identify with our people, we are more clever in talking and writing rather than in sharing in the problems and suffering of our people. True cross-bearing requires genuine identification with those who are suffering so we may bring about a change. This undertaking assumes that the one who moves to stand and participate in the suffering of others is in a better or healthier condition. The movement from one's secure life to identify with the helpless and the least involves an element of cross-bearing (suffering). There is a more powerful witness of the cross in this living act of identification with the helpless and the dispossessed than through merely sharing the spoken Word.

Almost everywhere in the world, people are looking for self-giving love, someone who will help them in their suffering and agony. There are many who live below the poverty line, especially in two-thirds of the world. They are homeless, hungry, sick, ignorant, naked, lonely, and in despair. We are living in Africa with AIDS patients in our communities and sometimes within our own families. Their orphans are on our thresholds. People displaced because of war and natural disasters such as drought and flood are among us. Those who literally beg for their daily bread are many. Those who can read and write are few. Is it possible to limit the message of the cross in such a situation simply to the verbal proclamation, "Jesus saves! He died for you!"? Definitely not! Jesus carried the cross by freeing people from their suffering and by working with them in their needs. We, as living members of the body of Jesus Christ, his church, should be involved without any restraint in solving these practical problems. This means that we have to sacrifice our time, talents, and treasures to make this happen. It means that we must engage in self-giving and sacrificial love in the discipleship of the cross.

The Cross and the Social System

Suffering that people endure socially is connected with their respective system of governance. A government that embezzles public treasures decreases the welfare of its citizens. Corruption, mismanagement, irresponsibility, dishonesty, segregation, ethnocentrism, racism, apartheid, and the like, when entrenched in the governing system, promote the suffering of the "others." Most of these systemic social evils have an element of selfishness. Selfishness and the cross are at variance. They are opposites. The cross is self-giving while corruption is self-aggrandizement. When established orders, whether civic or religious, use authority for their own selfish purpose, they promote the suffering of others. In objection to such a system, our Lord Jesus Christ spoke against the teachers of the law who embezzled from widows and did nothing out of a sense of justice, mercy, and faithfulness. The religious leaders of the time persecuted Jesus Christ not only for his benevolent deeds and miracles, which far surpassed theirs, but also because he vehemently opposed the showy and hypocritical system they had that did not address people's daily problems (Matthew 23:23). Our Lord disclosed the corruption, dishonesty, and unjust leadership of the Jewish ruling order. John the Baptist and Stephen followed in Christ's footsteps. They all paid with their lives for their opposition to an unjust leadership and for testifying to the truth, justice, mercy, and faithfulness of God.

In recent times Nelson Mandela was imprisoned for twenty-seven years for his stand against apartheid. Bishop Desmond Tutu raised a prophetic voice against the system. Many individuals in countries such as Uganda (during Idi Amin's regime), Ethiopia (during the Communist rule), and other African antions have paid with their lives by opposing the inhuman systems in their countries. These, however, are only a few examples. Systemic evil is rampant and stretches from the top to the bottom and from the center to the outskirts. This means that we Christians, disciples of the cross, have to stand against the systemic evil in our surroundings. We have to disclose these evils so justice, mercy, and faithfulness may prevail. This in turn may bring upon us the cross in its diverse modes: persecution, imprisonment, or even death. Despite what may come upon us, it is mandatory that we do not keep quiet when justice is overridden, the poor are trampled, and the innocent are sold. The theology of the cross in the African context demands such interference.

The cross of Christ, therefore, has a threefold relevance for us in Africa. First, it is the place where we are personally justified before God and have the hope of eternal life. Second, from our Lord's identification with the suffering and the disadvantaged, we get the impetus to do the same. Third, from our Lord's stand for justice, mercy, and faithfulness, we learn that we have an obligation to stand against injustice, corruption, and unfaithfulness in all its forms.

Theology of the Cross vs. Theology of Glory

Theology of the cross (*theologia crucis*) and theology of glory (*theologia gloriae*) are two phrases used by Dr. Martin Luther to distinguish between true theology and false theology. According to Luther, the essence of true theology is the theology of the cross. In the same manner he distinguishes between true theologians and false ones. He wrote:

> That person does not deserve to be called a theologian who looks upon the invisible things of God as though they were clearly perceptible in those things which have actually happened. He deserves to be called a theologian, however, who comprehends the visible and manifest things of God seen through suffering and the cross.[15]

---

15 *LW* 31:52. Cf. WA 1:361f. See also Paul Althaus, *The Theology of Martin Luther* (Philadelphia: Fortress, 1966), 25.

While a theology of glory knows God from his works, the theology of the cross knows him from his sufferings. Luther used *works* in a double sense. First, it meant God's work in creation, and second, it referred to humanity's good works intended to reach to God. When Luther used the word *sufferings*, he referred not only to Christ's suffering, but also to humanity's suffering. He makes the transition from the one to the other easily.

A theology of glory seeks to know God directly in his divine power, wisdom, and glory. The theology of the cross, on the other hand, finds God where he has hidden himself: in his sufferings, weakness, and foolishness. In the theology of the cross, "God's power appears not directly but paradoxically under helplessness and lowliness."[16] According to Luther, God's gifts and benefits are so hidden under the cross that unbelievers can neither see nor recognize them; instead, they consider them to be only trouble and disaster.[17]

First, we should not forget that the theology of the cross about which Luther gives witness has a soteriological dimension. In this, Luther's theology of the cross is similar to Paul's theology of the cross. Any human attempt to know or please God directly, either by human ethical achievements or metaphysical speculations, belongs to the theology of glory. The way to know God and to reeive forgiveness of sins is through faith in Christ crucified. Justification by faith alone for the sake of Christ crucified is not a matter to be negotiated. It is the Gospel (Galatians 1:8-10).

Having stated Luther's soteriological witness of the cross, how can we see the suffering we are going through in our world in light of the theology of the cross? Is God distant, unconcerned, impotent, or what? Not to mention what is happening elsewhere in the world, I will give some examples from Africa. Where is

---

16 Althaus, *Theology of Martin Luther*, 30.
17 Ibid., 30.

God when innocent children die with their mothers because of recurrent drought and famine, as has been the case in Ethiopia and the Horn of Africa? Where is God when innocent civilians are massacred because they belong to an ethnic group, as has been the case in the genocide in Rwanda? Where is God when flash flooding destroys farms, cattle, and life's earnings within an hour, as has occurred repeatedly in Mozambique. What about the nonstop war between Southern Sudan and Northern Sudan? After all, are not the South Sudanese Christians? Does not God stand even for his people?

If we look at this suffering in light of the theology of glory—that is, God in his power, might, and glory—it may lead one to deny the existence of a caring and benevolent God. It is only in light of the suffering God, who came to the world in the person of Jesus Christ, that we can make sense out of such an existence. In fact, our world, not only Africa, has witnessed a history of suffering century after century. There is no century in which suffering, either by epidemic, war, or natural calamity, has not been recorded. Are we certain that no such calamity—earthquake, war, or epidemic—will occur in the future? Are we so civilized that we can control natural and human catastrophic events?

How should we comprehend large-scale catastrophes that bring suffering to individuals, communities, nations, and the world at large? The suffering God, the God of the cross, can give us the answer. The God of the cross is not at all ignorant of the suffering of our world. Because he became an historical figure, bound to time and space, and because he himself suffered, he experienced all the dimensions of human suffering. Not only that, he stands with his suffering people, whatever the nature of the tribulation. The Lord who has cried, "My God, my God, why have you forsaken me?" (Matthew 27:46) stands close to all those who are in similar situations.

The Lord God, who has become an historical figure, bound to time and space in the person of our Lord Jesus Christ, does not view his suffering world as a spectator from the outside. He has suffered and still suffers together with his people on earth. The playlet entitled The *Long Silence* gives a dramatic and real presentation of human suffering in the world and God's place in this suffering. The setting is Judgment Day, and the people are arrayed before the throne of God. An animated discussion concerning God's ability to judge occurs. How can God judge the actions of individuals when he has not walked in their shoes? Finally, a representative group proposes that before God can be accepted as their judge, "he must endure what they had endured." The list of proposed tribulations includes illegitimacy, ethnic prejudice, injustice, torture, abandonment, and ultimately a horrible death. "And when the last had finished pronouncing sentence, there was a long silence. . . . For suddenly all knew that God had already served his sentence."[18]

The suffering of God in our Lord Jesus Christ makes it clear that God has not left us alone in our suffering. He himself has passed through it and is still passing through it. Let it be clear that our Lord does not promote suffering, nor does he want its permanency. According to Scripture, suffering entered our world because of sin. Our present world is a world suffering from the result and effects of sin. This is reality. Our God dealt with our suffering world neither by ignoring it nor by denying it. Rather, he entered its life of sin and suffering so he could redeem it. And Jesus Christ has done that through his death on the cross and the resurrection.

---

18 John R. W. Stott, *The Cross of Christ* (Downers Grove: InterVarsity, 1986), 336-337.

The Cross and Double Reconciliation

The cross of our Lord Jesus makes possible double reconciliation: vertical reconciliation with God and horizontal reconciliation with one another. Vertical reconciliation is effected when our conscience is made clean from the guilt of sin because of the blood our Lord shed on the cross. The author of the book of Hebrews, stating the power of the blood of Christ to reconcile us with God, writes:

> The blood of goats and bulls and the ashes of a heifer sprinkled on those who are ceremonially unclean sanctify them so that they are outwardly clean. How much more, then, will the blood of Christ, who through the eternal Spirit offered himself unblemished to God, cleanse our consciences from acts that lead to death, so that we may serve the living God! (Hebrews 9:13-14).

The reconciliation with God becomes the basis for the reconciliation with one another. For the sake of the death of our Lord Jesus Christ, God did not count our sins against us. He forgave us. A forgiven person has the impetus to forgive others. In fact, God forgave our sins though we deserved eternal punishment. If God forgave such an offense, should we not forgive one another? Therefore, God's forgiveness for the sake of Christ becomes the basis for reconciliation between human beings. As God made peace with us because of the cross of Christ, we can make peace with one another.

God's reconciliation with us for the sake of Christ and the peace thus made is especially relevant for Africa, where conflicts on ethnic, tribal, and national levels are rampant. The way God deals with us should be the norm for how we deal with one another. Each ethnic group, tribe, and nation can forgive the other for past offenses and can start a new relationship on the basis of justice. There should be willingness both by the offender and the offended to identify the causes for conflict. Once identified, the offense should be stopped and a proper compensation should be made. After the compensation there should be a resolve by both parties to live amicably in peace as equals and friends by maintaining the peace thus created. In this way the cross of Christ becomes not only the power for reconciliation, but also a model that human societies can imitate to solve conflicts.

The Cross and Eschatology

All human life culminates in death. As the Apostle Paul said, "The last enemy to be destroyed is death" (1 Corinthians 15:26). All other suffering can be considered as "elementary or minor" deaths because the greatest and last of all the sufferings is death. Our Lord went through that greatest suffering. After death no person can be accused by the Law because that person no longer lives. Our Lord died our death so the Law may not have power over us to accuse us. "Christ redeemed us from the curse of the Law by becoming a curse for us, for it is written: 'Cursed is everyone who is hung on a tree'" (Galatians 3:13).

In this sense the Christian's life is an eschatological life. Although Christians live on the earth bodily, they also share an eschatological life, the life of the resurrection. The Apostle Paul again says in describing this fact, "I have been crucified with Christ and I no longer live, but Christ lives in me. The life I live in the body, I live by faith in the Son of God, who loved me and gave himself for me. I do not set aside the grace of God, for if righteousness could be gained through the Law, Christ died for nothing!" (Galatians 2:20-21). Therefore, the cross of Christ enables the believer to share the new life, the life of the world to come, the life of righteousness and the kingdom of God. This "realized eschatology," however, reaches its final and complete stage when one passes from this world of time and space to the next world. Not only human beings wait for the final and complete consummation, where the limitations of time and space cannot hinder. The whole creation eagerly is waiting for that day (Romans 8:18-22).

Conclusion

The cross of Christ has a multifaceted and holistic relevance on personal, communal, national, and cosmic levels. For those who have the eye to see and the sense to understand its meaning, over and beyond its apparent weakness, the cross gives the ultimate answer to the human quest. In fact, it is the answer for understanding reality and our existence. It is through the cross of Christ and his resurrection that we can make sense of he present world and our own existence. The cross of Christ and his resurrection gives us hope amid suffering and a seemingly hopeless world (Romans 8:31-39). The theology of the cross gives us the motivation to work positively for righteousness, peace, and reconciliation. In short, it is the heartbeat and center of our existence. The cross is the most important signpost for our witness in the twenty-first century. That is why the Apostle Paul confessed, "For I resolved to know nothing while I was with you except Jesus Christ and him crucified" (1 Corinthians 2:2).

For Further Reading

Adeyemo, Tokunboh. *Salvation in African Tradition*. Nairobi: Evangel, 1979.

Althaus, Paul. *The Theology of Martin Luther*. Philadelphia: Fortress, 1966.

Aulén, Gustaf. *Christus Victor*. New York: Macmillan, 1969.

Gruchy, John W. and Charles Villa-Vicencio, eds. *Doing Theology in Context: South African Perspectives*. Vol. 1. Maryknoll: Orbis; Cape Town: David Philip, 1994.

Hengel, Martin. *Crucifixion in the Ancient World and the Folly of the Message of the Cross*. Philadelphia: Fortress, 1977.

Kinoti, Hannah W. and John M. Waliggo, eds. *The Bible in African Christianity*. Nairobi: Acton, 1997.

Mbiti, John S. *Introduction to African Religion*. 2nd edition. Nairobi: East African Education Publishers, 1991.

Parratt, John, ed. *A Reader in African Christian Theology*. London: SPCK, 1987.

Stott, John R. W. *The Cross of Christ*. Downers Grove: InterVarsity, 1986.

_____. *Issues Facing Christians Today*. 2nd ed. London: Marshall Pickering, 1990.

Confessing Christ in the Apostles' Creed

The Apostles' Creed is the shortest of the three ecumenical creeds which have reached us from the ancient church.[1] Through the message of its content, it has touched the lives of innumerable men and women throughout the centuries. As a result some have even called it the "Bible in miniature." The great reformer of the sixteenth century, Martin Luther, said the following concerning it while delivering a sermon:

> This confession we did not devise, nor did the fathers of former times. As the bee collects honey from many fair and gay flowers, so is this Creed collected, in appropriate brevity, from the books of the beloved prophets and apostles—from the entire Holy Scriptures. It is fittingly called the "Apostles' Symbol" or "Apostles' Creed." For brevity and clearness it could not have been better arranged, and it has remained in the church from the ancient time. It must either have been composed by the apostles themselves or it was collected from their writings and sermons by their ablest disciples.[2]

---

[1] Adapted from a paper read at the 13th General Assembly of the Ethiopian Evangelical Church Mekane Yesus, January 1989.

[2] *Luther's Works*, Vol. IX, 16-23; H. T. Kerr, ed., *A Compendium of Luther's Theology* (Philadelphia: Fortress, 1966), 39-40. Cf. also for a similar idea, *The Book of Concord*, translated by T. G. Tappert (Philadelphia: Fortress, 1959), 363.

In 1537, in order to bear witness to his opponents that he held "to the real Christian church," which until then had preserved the three symbols or creeds, he issued a short pamphlet entitled "The Three Symbols or Creeds of the Christian Faith." There, Luther remarked: "The first Symbol, that of the Apostles, is truly the finest of all. Briefly, correctly, and in a splendid way it summarizes the articles of faith."[3]

The above assessment by the Reformer would suffice in witness to the value and nature of the Apostles' Creed. As correctly evaluated, it is brief and biblical. What about its origin and usage?

Until the fifteenth century, the Apostles' Creed was taken to have come from the Apostles. This is based on a tradition which is believed to have been in existence at the latest from the fourth century. The tradition as recorded by Tyrannius Rufinus (A.D. 345-410) says:

> As the [Apostles] were therefore on the point of taking leave of each other, they first settled an agreed norm for their future preaching, so that they might not find themselves, widely separated as they would be, giving out different doctrines to the people they invited to believe in Christ. So they met together in one spot and, being filled with the Holy Spirit, compiled their brief token, as I have said, of their future preaching, each making the contribution he thought fit; and they decreed that it should be handed out as standard teaching to believers.

The above description of Rufinus may well be a remote and exaggerated report of a fact which might have actually happened as we shall see below.

---

[3] L. W. Spitz, ed., "M. Luther" in *Luther's Works*, 55 Vols. (Philadelphia: Muhlenberg, 1960), 34:201; P. Althous, *The Theology of Martin Luther*, trans. by R. C. Shultz (Philadelphia: Fortress, 1966), 7.

Since the work of Laurentius Valla (A.D. 1404/5-1457), a propagator of Renaissance ideas in the fifteenth century, the above testimony of Rufinus has been taken to be legendary and false. Under the influence of the Renaissance and humanism, as exemplified by Valla, it has been the legacy of the Western mind to doubt and criticize whatever had been handed down from the ancients, including the Holy Scriptures. However, we have to weigh the conclusions of such skepticism very cautiously as the perverted reason naturally is an ally neither of faith, nor of the truth connected with it. By this I do not mean that we have blindly to support the ancients and their traditions no matter what the evidence of our investigations demonstrate. Rather, we have to weight carefully the results to determine whether they are conclusive in disproving a tradition that has been received for over fifteen centuries. Any evidence, whether internal or external, which supports the tradition, which locates the origin of the Apostles' Creed in the apostolic circles, is a plus for the claim of the tradition. Let us review the available evidence to this end.

First of all, there is hardly any scholar who doubts the apostolic authenticity of the Apostles' Creed as to its content. All of its assertions are biblical and can be supported by the apostolic teachings and preachings in the New Testament documents. This is a plus for the tradition and needs no further elaboration.

More than this, however, there are external evidences that would point to the fact that the creed in its basic form may go back substantially to the apostolic circles and their environment. It may be that the declaratory form of the Apostles' Creed known to us is from the fourth, or fifth, or even eighth century. However, there are creeds substantially the same as the Apostles' Creed which go back to the second and third century, which were believed by the whole church to have come from the apostles.

Among these creeds is found what is known as the "Rule of Faith." Before stating the content of the "Rule of Faith," Irenaeus (c. A.D. 190) prefixes the following comment: "The church, though dispersed throughout the whole world, even to the ends of the earth, has received from the apostles and their disciples this faith." After that Irenaeus presents his version of the "Rule of Faith" in the following words:

> [The church believes] in one God, the Father Almighty, maker of heaven, and earth, and the sea and all things that are in them; and in one Christ Jesus, the Son of God, who became incarnate for our salvation; and in the Holy Spirit, who proclaimed through prophets the dispensations of God, and the advents, and the birth from a virgin, and the passion, and the resurrection from the dead, and the ascension into heaven in the flesh of the beloved Christ Jesus, our Lord, and His manifestation from heaven in the glory of the Father.

Tertullian (c. A.D. 200) for his part gives the following version of the "Rule of Faith," which he says "has come down from the beginning of the Gospel":

> We . . . believe in one only God, yet subject to this dispensation that the one only God has also a Son, his Word who has proceeded from himself, by whom all things were made and without whom nothing has been made: that this [Son] was sent by the Father into the virgin and was born of her both man and God, Son of man and Son of God, and was named Jesus Christ: that he suffered, died, and was buried, according to the Scriptures, and having been raised up by the Father and taken back into heaven, sits at the right hand of the Father and will come to judge the quick and the dead: and that thereafter he, according to his promise, sent from the Father the

Holy Spirit the Paraclete, the sanctifier of the faith of those who believe in the Father and the Son and the Holy Spirit.

Whether both Irenaeus and Tertullian reproduced the "Rule of Faith" exactly, or made a free reproduction is not very clear, but from the context and the manner of writing it seems to be a free reproduction. In spite of this, we can see that there is a considerable similarity between the "Rule of Faith" as presented by Irenaeus or by Tertullian and the Apostles' Creed as we have it, as to both form and substance. This similarity is not to be taken lightly.

If one can claim apostolic origin for the "Rule of Faith," as both Irenaeus and Tertullian assume, there is no reason that the creed which is almost identical with it in its main substance could not also be apostolic. In fact, the difference between the "Rule of Faith" and the Apostles' Creed seems to reflect only local variations. While the Apostles' Creed is a Roman creed based on the old Roman Symbol, the "Rule of Faith" was the same creed with some variations according to locality. In his commentary on the Apostles' Creed, Tyrannius Rufinus confirms this fact when he writes:

> I think it appropriate to mention that certain additions are to be found in this article in some churches. No such development, however, can be detected in the case of the church of the city of Rome. . . . The ancient custom is maintained there whereby candidates who are on the point of receiving the grace of baptism deliver the creed publicly, in the hearing of the congregation of the faithful. As a result, since those who have preceded them in the faith are listening attentively, the interpolation of even a simple is not tolerated.

If this is the case, we can believe that the Apostles' Creed as we have it today can be traced ultimately to the pure Roman

Symbol, which in turn as the "Rule of Faith" was of apostolic origin, as Irenaeus and Tertullian testify.

Another evidence which points to the apostolic origin of the Apostles' Creed is the setting of the interrogatory creed contained in the so-called "Apostolic Tradition" of Hippolytus. This interrogatory creed of Hippolytus (c. A.D. 215) is found as an integral part of the baptismal rite which was derived from the rite of Jewish proselytes. The baptismal rite, the eucharist, as well as the Agape rites in Hippolytus were equally Judaic. As Dix puts it, there is scarcely one element in the cultus as described by Hippolytus for which clear Jewish parallels cannot be found."

If this is the case, where would such a concentration of Jewish Christians be found, who might have developed this statement which contains the Creed on the model of proselyte baptism? Clearly this evidence points to an early date and to the Jerusalem church. The existence of the creed within such manifestly Jewish clothing is a major plus for the claim of the tradition.

The fact that we cannot point to a specific date of composition for the Apostles' Creed as we can for the Nicene Creed and the Athanasian Creed, also supports the statement of Tertullian that the creed emerged from the "beginning of the gospel."

On the basis of the above evidences we believe that the creed initially originated in the apostolic circles and finally reached its present form, in the process leaving several local variations. Assuming then the apostolic origin of the creed, we will now proceed to consider the christological confession of that creed.

The Christ in the Apostles' Creed

The confession about Jesus Christ is found in the second article of the creed. In reality, the second article should have been given the first place, because our understanding of the first and third articles as well as the whole of our Christian faith depends on our correct understanding of its content. Karl Barth, while describing the second article, wrote:

> Whether a sermon and proclamation in word or writing have rightly or wrongly a place in the Christian church is decided by their relationship to the second article.[4]

The second article is saturated with christological designations. Every word and phrase is saturated with Christ and his deeds. Let us consider some of the principal phrases.

"And I believe in Jesus."

The name "Jesus" is an anglicized form of the Septuagint rendering for the Hebrew Yeshua. In the first instance, the name "Jesus" is an express of his humanity; there were many others who bore the name "Jesus" both in the time of our Lord and even up to the beginning of the second century A.D.[5] In order to distinguish the "Jesus" of the Gospel from others, the Gospels sometimes used adjectives such as "from Nazareth of Galilee" or "Nazarene" (Matthew 21:11; Mark 10:47; John 1:45). After the beginning of the second century A.D., the name "Jesus" seems to have been consciously avoided by other persons and was retained only for our Lord.[6]

The name is much more than a mere express of his humanity. It was not an accident that both Matthew and Luke write in the annunciation "and you shall call his name Jesus . . . for he will save his people from their sins" (Matthew 1:21; Luke 1:31). It was a name chosen from above and sent through a messenger.

---

4 K. Barth, *Credo* (New York: Scribner's, 1962), 39.
5 G. Kittel, ed., *Theological Dictionary of the New Testament* (Grand Rapids: Eerdmans, 1965), 3:285-286.
6 Ibid., 287.

This is all the more significant when we investigate the roots of the name "Jesus."

The Hebrew form of the name "Jesus" represents a form of the divine name *Yahweh* together with a subsidiary form of the Hebrew verb which means "to save," or "to help." If we put together the two parts, the root could be rendered as "*Yahweh* saves or helps," thus "Jesus" means "*Yahweh* saves."

The connection of the name "Jesus" with "*Yahweh*," even in its root form, cannot be taken lightly. It directs us to the fact that Jesus himself is *Yahweh*—i.e., *Yahweh* who saves. This unity of Jesus with *Yahweh* (though not in person) speaks against those who teach that Jesus is somewhat inferior to *Yahweh*, the Creator.

"I believe in . . . Christ."

The Greek title *Christos*, which later became a proper name for Jesus, is equivalent to the Hebrew *Mashiach*, which means "the anointed one." We know that in the Old Testament times priests, prophets, and kings were "anointed." We will here concentrate on the kingship aspect of Jesus in his designation as *Mashiach*, i.e., "Christ, the anointed one."

The Jews after the destruction of their state, especially when they were in exile, looked forward to the fulfillment of the promise of God to David in 2 Samuel 7:12ff:

> When your days are fulfilled and you lie down with your fathers, I will raise up your offspring after you, who shall come forth from your body, and I will establish his kingdom. . . . And your house and your kingdom shall be made sure forever before me; your throne shall be established forever.

On the basis of this, they held that they would be receiving a king anointed by God, from the seed of David, who would restore the Kingdom of Israel. Even though the Jewish concept of the coming *Mashiach* shows some variations, the predominant view was that he would be a political Messiah, with full grandeur and earthly power. It is questionable whether the Jews understood the correct sense of the divine promise from the start, since Jesus rebuked them once, saying: "You know neither the Scriptures nor the power of God" (Matthew 22:29).

The Jesus of the Gospels, however, though he accepted the title "Christ" when others confessed about him, never accepted it in the sense understood by the Jews; that is, as a political and nationalistic leader. Even the disciples did not understand the real nature of his messiahship at the beginning. Thus, when Jesus told them about his suffering, we see Peter rebuking him (Mark 8:33). And Jesus, rebuking Peter, said, "Get behind me, Satan! For you are not on the side of God but of men." Oscar Cullmann writes:

> This means nothing less than that Jesus considered as a satanic temptation the conception of the Messiah which Peter implied by his rebuke.[7]

Jesus did not openly use this title about himself as he did other titles such as the "Son of Man," because the popular idea of the day about the Messiah was incompatible with his own mission. Jesus did not come to show his own grandeur and temporal power as would be expected from a political Messiah. As he confessed before Pilate, his kingship was not of this world. It was with the same understanding that he rejected the temptation in the wilderness when the devil showed him "all the kingdoms of the world and the glory of them" (Matthew 4:8).

The devil lurks about constantly attempting to snare the church, the body of Christ on earth, with the same temptation. Members of the church, including its leadership, can fall into this

---

7 O. Cullmann, *The Christology of the New Testament* (Philadelphia: Westminster, 1963), 122.

specific snare. Forgetting the real nature of Christ's mission, expressed in his service and his cross, the church has tried to climb up the ladder to hold temporal power. Not to mention some manifestations in the church of today, the church of the Middle Ages in Europe showed an ambition for absolute authority on earth. The result of this ambition was an utter decay and worldliness in the life of the church, which in turn led to the Reformation. It is then important for us, the body of Christ, to have the mind of Christ which was manifested to us in his service and the cross (Philippians 2:5-11).

"I believe in . . . his only Son."[8]

The title "Son of God" was not unfamiliar in the Hellenistic world. In Hellenism, anyone who was believed to possess some kind of divine power was called "Son of God" by others, or gave himself the title. Miracle worker were also called "Sons of God."[9] Some scholars have ventured to suggest that the title "Son of God" applied to Jesus in the New Testament has come from the Hellenistic use of the title. This, however, is an erroneous conclusion reached without a thorough understanding of the similarity and differences between the use of that title in the New Testament and in the Hellenistic world.

In the Hellenistic understanding, the designation "Son of God" can hardly be separated from the polytheistic background of pagan antiquity, whereas in the New Testament Jesus is the Son of the one God, undertood within a monotheistic setting. In addition, as indicated above, the designation "Son of God" was given to those in the Hellenistic world if they were believed to

---

8 This is one of the witnesses to the antiquity of the Apostles' Creed. We do not here find developed qualifications regarding the Son, such as "begotten, not made," "of one essence," etc., as we do in the Nicene Creed (A.D. 325) and thereafter.

9 O. Cullmann, op. cit, 272.

have the gift of divine powers and doing miracles. However, the most important passages of the Synoptic Gospels in which Jesus appears as the Son of God show him precisely not as a miracle worker like many others, but as one radically and uniquely distinguished from all other men. This title means to Jesus, not primarily miraculous power, but absolute obedience of a son in the execution of a divine commission. To Jesus, the most important thing as the "Son of God" was doing the will of the Father, not going around doing miracles to manifest his greatness and divine power; for example, when Satan tempted him saying, "If you are the Son of God . . ." (Matthew 4:1-11), Jesus would not resort to miracles to prove his sonship, as suggested by Satan. It is highly significant that Jesus here rejects as satanic the Hellenistic conception of his divine sonship in the sense of miraculous powers.

The point of the temptation is not whether Jesus believes that God's miraculous power is present in the Son, but whether he will be disobedient to his Father by attempting to use that power apart from the fulfillment of his specific commission as the Son, because the sonship of Jesus was based on the complete unity of his will with the Father. He not only obeyed him when he was granted divine power to do miracles, but also when he was "given up" and "forsaken" by the Father, so that through his suffering and death many should be saved. The prayer in Gethsemane, "My Father . . . not as I will but as thou wilt," shows his complete obedience and sonship.

In addition, in New Testament understanding, Jesus' sonship was unique; it was not in the sense that all men are children of God. Matthew and Luke describe his virgin birth through the Holy Spirit, thus showing thr uniqueness of his sonship. John shows Jesus' unique sonship by asserting his unique origin. He writes, "No one has ever see God; the only Son, who is in the bosom of the Father, he has made him known" (John 1:18). The author of Hebrews also clearly affirms the unique relation of Jesus with God: "In many and various ways God spoke of old to our fathers by the prophets; but in these last days he has spoken to us by a Son, whom he appointed. . ." (Hebrews 1:1). This clearly shows that Jesus was not seen as another of the prophets who also used to do miracles, but as a unique Son who had a special relationship with his Father.

We Christians who make up the body of Christ, the church, are given the power to become children of God. Our sonship, however, is by adoption, while that of Jesus was by birth. Nevertheless, the church must learn from the attitude of Jesus towards his status as "Son," manifested in doing the will of his Father, whether it was the joy of transfiguration or the agony of the cross. For Jesus, his food was doing the will of his Father. We may ask what is the guiding principle of the church today? Whose will is the church striving to fulfil? Its own? The world's? Or the will of God?

From the attitude of Jesus, it is quite clear that the church as his body ought to fulfil not its own will, nor that of the world, but the will of God as revealed in the Scriptures. The will of God revealed in the Scriptures should be the church's norm and the guiding spirit in all its actions and resolutions. If the will of God was food for Christ, who is and was the head of the church, how much more should it be for the church which is his body.

According to the tradition of the Reformers, the two marks of a true church are the Scripture and the Sacraments. Where the word of God is preached, taught, and obeyed in its purity, and where the Sacraments, the visible words, are administered correctly, there the church exists. Other philanthropic deeds of the church are, and should be, the fruits of its faith in the Word, who showed us *Caritas Dei*, the love of God. For the church to put philanthropy in the forefront and to forget the Word of God, the very source from which it is nourished, will definitely lead the church to a loss of its identity, as well as to a loss of the cherished philanthropy. Thus, the present church should consider whether it performs the duties which it thinks ought to be done, or whether it does what is the inevitable outcome of its faith in the Word of God.

"Suffered under Pontius Pilate, was crucified, dead and buried"

Pontius Pilate (A.D. 26-36), who followed Valerius Gratus, was the fifth officer of the Roman Empire to be in charge of Judea after the birth of Jesus.[10] It is important to note that Pilate was a local governor. The mentioning of Pilate in the creed informs us that Jesus lived and died for us in a specific period and place in the history of the world. In short, it shows us that Jesus was a figure in history. Attempts which have been made to disprove the historical fact of Christ during the past 200 years have failed. The historical fact of Christ is now incontrovertibly established. The fact that extant secular records of the first hundred years contain only a few references was because Christianity at first was considered as one of many religious cults originating in the East, so that there was little in it to attract pagan historians. Their attention was directed to it when it came into conflict with the state. The earliest pagan writers who refer to Christianity in such a context significantly mention Christ as its founder.[11]

Jesus, after having completed his mission on earth, now sits at the right hand of his Almighty Father. Yet the church as his body lives in history as a tangible reality. The attitudes of the earthly Jesus towards the local rulers of governments (such as Pilate) are, therefore, determinative for the church.

---

10 M. C. Tenney, *New Testament Survey* (Grand Rapids: Eerdmans, 1961), 428.
11 Tacitus, *Annals* XV. 44; Suetonius, *Claudius* 25, Nero 16; Pliny, *Epistles* X. 96. Cf. "Jesus Christ" in *The New Bible Dictionary*, edited by J. D. Douglas (Leicester: Inter-Varsity, 1962); Tenney, 199-201.

It is instructive that the fate of Jesus was decided by the decrees and verdicts of the local and earthly rulers. His birth happened to be far from his home, due to a decree from Augustus Caesar. He had to flee to Egypt in his infancy due to Herod the Great (37-4 B.C.). And at last he was crucified under the verdict given by Pontius Pilate, a Gentile representative of the Roman Empire.[12] Jesus had either to deal with or submit himself to their verdicts, yet he knew that ultimately the verdict was not from them, but from his Father in heaven. That was the reason that he answered to Pilate, "You would have no power over me unless it had been given to you from above" (John 19:11).

The church too cannot be negligent of the earthly powers and rulers around it in every place and age. As an historical figure, the church has either to deal with, or to submit to, the decrees and verdicts of the local rulers at all stages of its pilgrimage. Thus, the earthly fate of the church is in a way tied up with the kind of government and rulers in its locality. Under whatever kind of government or local rulers or earthly situation the church lives, that does not in any way minimize it being the body of Christ. Thus, the church has to learn to deal with and be prepared to give an appropriate answer while in its existence on earth with the earthly rulers. Yet just as was the case with Jesus, whatever kind of encounter the church may have with the local rulers, it should know that the ultimate power lies with God, that no ruler shall have power over the church unless he is given this from above.

"Suffered"

The historical and true suffering of Christ, demonstrated in his agony on the cross, is where God spoke to humankind in the loudest voice he could. The suffering and the cross of Christ revealed to the world the inmost nature of God, the very heart of

---

12 Cf. "Pilate" in *The New Bible Dictonary*.

God, his inexplicable and immeasurable love. God could not have spoken any better to the world than he did on the cross. Yet this has always remained a dilemma and stumbling block to the world which always likes to focus its attention on temporal and transient glory. Nevertheless, to those who have realized the transient nature of this world, the cross of Christ is full of meaning. Indeed for them it is the gate to everlasting glory.

Unfortunately, the suffering and the cross of Christ, which have been a stumbling block to the world, possess the very key by which the world itself could be meaningful and sensible. How can we account for and get meaning out of the various manifestations of suffering which we see occurring in our world every day? Famine, wars, epidemics, pestilence, deadly viruses, and poverty are just some of the manifestations of this suffering. Is the world then doomed to such sufferings hopelessly? Is not there hope for humanity? Or does suffering have the final word?

The suffering and pain in the world make sense only when viewed from the perspective of the suffering of Christ. The suffering and pain in the world are the result of sin. However, humanity is not all alone in passing through these sufferings. The very God who created the universe and man has passed through the same suffering. He bore "the sins of the whole world," thus passing through the worst, the maximum suffering of which one can think. As the apostle put it, "though he was in the form of God . . . he humbled himself and became obedient until death, even death on the cross" (Philippians 2:6-8). It is a great privilege to humanity and a key for its self-understanding and existence to know that there is a God who has suffered and suffers for him and with him. The God revealed in Jesus Christ is, first of all, not a God who invites suffering. But when suffering comes, as is the case in our world, he does not evade it or flee from it. Rather he passes through it victoriously. In the same way, he helps his children not to flee the world and its suffering, but to pass through them refined as gold. He clearly stated this fact when he said, "In the world you have tribulation; but be of good cheer, I have overcome the world" (John 16:33).

The function of the church then, as the body of Christ living in the suffering world, is to bring to light the God who suffered for all, so that humanity may not live in ignorance, as if suffering, pain, and sin were unconquered powers. Just as Paul exclaimed, "O death, where is thy victory? O death, where is thy sting? Thanks be to God, who gives us the victory through our Lord Jesus Christ," so the church too can proclaim the victory won by Jesus over suffering and pain, both in its words and in its deeds. Thus, the church in reality becomes in Christ the hope of the world, the instrument for the redemption of humanity.

"On the third day he rose again from the dead, ascended to heaven, sits at the right hand of God the Father Almighty; thence he will come to judge the living and the dead."

The resurrection of Christ is the foundation on which the church is established. The affirmation by the author of Hebrews, "Jesus Christ is the same yesterday, today, and forever" (Hebrews 13:8), presupposes the resurrection of Christ. If Jesus were dead, there is no way he could be the same yesterday, today, and forever. As the Apostle Paul wrote, "If Christ has not been raised, then our preaching is in vain and your faith is in vain" (1 Corinthians 15:14). Similarly, we can also say if Christ has not been raised, then our church and all we do in Christ's name is in vain. "But in fact, Christ has been raised from the dead, the first fruits of those who have fallen asleep."

If the cross, suffering, and death were the end of Jesus, then they would have been the master of the world. But now, through the resurrection of Jesus Christ, "death is swallowed up in victory," therefore, the church should conduct its affairs with the realization and confidence that the risen Christ is present in its midst. This risen Christ, who sits at the right hand of God, with the token that he has completed all his work to be done on earth, will come the second time to give his verdict of justice. Till then he works, in his Spirit, with his church on earth. This is the Christ whom we confess in the Apostles' Creed.

Christian Faith in the New Millennium

At the end of the present millennium we find peoples of the world with their different cultures opening up to each other. Peoples and cultures of the world are not as remote from each other as they used to be in the first century or even in the last century. Modern communication systems bring people from every corner of the world to individual homes even if the people themselves do not have a chance to travel. As it often has been said, we live more and more in a "global village." Even if the term village may sound a bit exaggerated, we can feel that there is something unifying or identifying the peoples of the earth with each other as if they belonged to one nation.

On the other hand, in spite of all that brings the people of the earth closer to each other, their unique cultural and social heritage still remains. This makes wondering at and learning from each other an enjoyable possibility. The new millennium into which we are entering is at the threshold of these phenomena. What kind of Christian faith do we then expect to live and confess in this new millennium? As far as I am concerned the Christian faith in the new millennium should demonstrate the following two major things: Continuity in the apostolic faith and concern for each other, especially the poor.

Continuity in the Apostolic Faith

For us the year 2000 may represent too long a period of time. We feel that the world has a very long history and that we have progressed very far. Midnight on the last day of December 1999 will be not only the start of a new year but also of a new millennium. So people are waiting for the day with much expectation and with a sense of great accomplishment and progress. If seen from the biblical perspective, however, the period leading up to the year 2000 cannot be considered very long. "With the Lord a day is like a thousand years, and a thousand years are like a day" (2 Peter 3:8). We may be just finishing our second day and entering our third day from the perspective of the Lord. This demonstrates the fact that we have to follow the same faith as that of the apostles and their disciples without exaggerating our remoteness or distance of time from them.

The apostolic faith exists regardless of place and time.

One of the marks of true followers of Jesus Christ is continuity in his teachings and that of the apostles. "He who receives you receives me, and he who receives me receives the one who sent me" (Matthew 10:40). The Apostle Paul praised the young Timothy for the knowledge of his teaching, way of life, purpose, faith, and patience, etc., and admonishes Timothy to continue in what he has learned (2 Timothy 3:10-17). The first believers who gave themselves to the Lord after hearing the message preached by St. Peter devoted themselves to the apostles' teaching and the fellowship, to the breaking of bread and to prayer (Acts 2:41-42). It is the same faith that we who are living at the threshold of the new millennium are following, committed to, and intend to carry on.

It is very important for us to ascertain whether the faith we hold, which we preach in our churches and teach in our theological schools and faculty, has continuity with the apostolic faith or not. The true Christian church has one faith, one Lord, and one baptism (Ephesians 4:5). The content of that faith does not change with time or place.

The famous church father, Irenaeus, once wrote the following about the permanence of the apostolic faith in his work entitled *Against Heresies*: "The Church though dispersed throughout the whole world, even to the ends of the earth, has received from the apostles and their disciples this faith. . . ." Then, after describing the content of the faith in words very similar to the Apostles' Creed, he continues:

> As I have already observed, the Church, having received this preaching and this faith, although scattered throughout the whole world, yet, as if occupying but one house, carefully preserves it. She also believes these points of doctrine just as if she had but one soul, and one and the same heart, and she proclaims them, and teaches them, and hands them down, with perfect harmony, as if she possessed only one mouth. For, although the languages of the world are dissimilar, yet the import of the tradition is one and the same. . . . Nor will any one of the rulers in the churches, however highly gifted he may be in point of eloquence, teach doctrines different from these (for no one is greater than the Master); nor, on the other hand, will he who is deficient in power of expression inflict injury on tradition. For the faith being ever one and the same, neither does one who is able at great length to discourse regarding it make any addition to it, nor does one who can say but little diminish it (Irenaeus, *Against Heresies*, 1:10).

If we really believe in the communion of saints, as we usually confess, we cannot but have the same faith as the early church. The content of the faith was handed on by the Lord to his first disciples and by the disciples to their followers. Christians of the first millennium handed on the same faith to those of the second millennium. We who are now living at the end of the second millennium have to carry over the same faith and hand it on to the generations of the third millennium. Christianity is not created anew in every generation or century. Rather it is newly experienced by each generation. The fish has been there in the sea for thousands of years. But each time we eat, we experience its taste and nourishment. It is similar with Christianity.

The apostolic faith may be contextualized by cannot be modified or changed.

In recent years there has been a good understanding of the need to respect cultures and people groups. As a result genuine attempts have been made to share the message of Jesus Christ without imposing one's culture upon the recipients. On the other hand, some have gone to the point of modifying or changing the very content and message of the faith in order to speak to contemporary culture. It is very important to note here that there is no culture in the past, present, or future to which Christianity will not be relevant. In fact, though the forms and expressions may change from place to place or from time to time, the situation, needs, and predicaments of human beings are the same throughout the centuries and will remain the same until one gets an answer by faith in Jesus Christ. In my own judgment, there is no substantial difference , even between the so-called modern and scientific world and the world of the first century when it comes to the essential questions of human destiny. The difference I see between the two worlds is only that of "mechanical advantage."

Christianity deals with the question of relationships—a right relationship with God and man. There is an inner-most yearning for this right relationship in everybody, whether a scientist in his laboratory or an illiterate farmer in a remote bush. I heard once of the death of two doctors in a renowned research laboratory.

When the news of their death was revealed, it was told that the one killed the other and then himself due to a quarrel they had. Thus we see that love, forgiveness, joy, and peace are needed for every human being and every place in the world, regardless of one's background, such as country, education, occupation, or culture. No sophistication of the modern world, the digital system, computerization, or automation of any kind can help human beings in the area of relationships. The only one who can help is Jesus Christ, the Son of God, who has opened the way to a right relationship with God and fellow human beings with his death on the cross that heralded love, forgiveness, and reconciliation. I once also saw a rich man living in a big house with a lot of material wealth in it. However, he was alone and lonely. I later on came to realize that he no longer lived with his wife because of the poor relationship they had. I said in my heart, "It is much better for a person to live with his wife (a person) in love, forgiveness, and patience than to live alone in a big stone house with all material wealth in it." A right personal relationship both with God and one's fellow man is a key to understanding what Christianity is all about. As I understand it, this right relationship does not conflict in any way with scientific progress or advancement. As air, food, and water are needed for every human being, regardless of his background, so also true love, forgiveness, and fellowship are needed for all. They are found by faith in him who is "the Way, the Truth, and the Life." It is this faith that we need as we enter into the new millennium.

The apostolic faith accepts the lordship of Jesus Christ and the authority of his Word.

The Apostle Paul writes about Jesus Christ, "And he is the head of the body, the church; he is the beginning and the firstborn from among the dead, so that in everything he might have the supremacy" (Colossians 1:18). Accepting the lordship and supremacy of Jesus Christ is demonstrated by obedience to him and his Word. He who does not accept his Word cannot accept him. There is no dichotomy between his Word and himself. I have heard a number of comments from church members that some churches preach politics from the pulpit, leaving aside the Word of God. If that is true, those churches have forgotten their calling and mission. A church that does not have a message from the Word of God to its audience is like a gun without a bullet. It is important to remember at this point what the reformer Luther said about the two marks of a true church, namely the right preaching and teaching of the Word of God and the right administration of the Sacraments. Whatever may be said to elucidate the message, Jesus Christ and his Word should have full authority in our churches. Our acceptance of the lordship of Jesus Christ and the authority of his Word should be demonstrated in both our churches and daily life. The modern church, if she wants to keep her identity with the Apostolic Church, needs to live in the same faith, and preach and teach the same faith.

The apostolic faith is mission oriented.

The church all over the world is the result of mission. To learn this we simply need to go back and read our history. The first missionary was our Lord Jesus Christ, who was sent from his Father. Ever since his first coming, mission has been going on. We may explain mission with different words and understand it in many ways. But for me, mission is the very breath of the church. It is her confession, telling who she is, what she believes, and why she believes it. In short, it is telling what Christ has meant for her and what he promises to do for those who believe in him. This kind of mission cannot be limited to a certain designated locality. It starts first with one's life, then family and friends, neighbors, and one's town and country. It involved one's total existence and way of life. It is impossible to evangelize others without first being ourselves evangelized. He who does not know and has never experienced the blessings of Jesus Christ in his own life and church cannot offer to others a genuine invitation to share in the blessing. It will be sheet hypocrisy to do that.

Inspired individuals and groups have done a great deal to give testimony to their faith in unreached areas all over the world. But in some of the countries which were seed beds of missionaries, the very faith of the church is under attack. People have turned their eyes to material enticements and worldly pleasures, forgetting that whatever is material is temporary. The name "Christian" is left merely as an historical relic and tradition without any demonstration of the essential substance of Christianity, which is living faith in Jesus Christ. In view of this, the traditional and customary thinking of doing mission in certain designated areas, such as Africa, Asia, and Latin America, is painful to me. At this stage in history, I am quite convinced that mission and the proclamation of the saving power of Jesus Christ are needed everywhere with almost equal urgency. With the Apostle Paul we should be able to say, "I am obligated both to Greeks and non-Greeks, both to the wise and the foolish. That is why I am so eager to preach the gospel also to you who are at Rome. I am not ashamed of the gospel, because it is the power of God for the salvation of everyone who believes. . . ." Everyone who believes in the message of the gospel will be saved. So mission should be done everywhere, among all nations (Matthew 28:19-20).

Concern for Each Other, Especially the Poor

One of the marks of true disciples of Jesus Christ is love. Love cannot be love if it is not translated into action. The Apostle John writes, "If anyone has material possessions and sees his brother in need but has no pity in him, how can the love of God be in him? Dear children, let us not love with words or tongue, but with actions and in truth" (1 John 3:17-18). Love requires interaction. It cannot take place in seclusion or isolation. The present seclusion and individualism seen in some cultures should be weighed carefully on the basis of this concept of love. We have heard and read a number of times of people dying in their apartments and their bodies being found after a number of weeks. It is very sad to learn that nobody ever visited them regularly. The church should be the foremost example of the love of Jesus Christ both within her members and in the community among whom she exists and whom she serves. Jesus Christ sought the lost, the downcast, and the marginalized. So should his church on earth. It is expected from the body of Christ, the church, to reflect him who is love. He gave not only his possessions, honor, etc., but also his very life in love.

Conclusion: We expect and hope for the coming of our Lord and Savior Jesus Christ.

The present world around us is full of evil. When we see the countries in the world arena, materially affluent nations seem to be selfish, greedy, and protective of their own advantages. On the other hand, materially poorer nations seem to be torn with discord, war, and envy. What then is the hope for our world in the years to come and particularly in the new millennium? If all the nations of the world were to be led by the Spirit of Jesus Christ, who was born from the virgin Mary, suffered under Pontius Pilate, was crucified, died, and was buried, then rose on the third day from death, the world would be a peaceful place. There would be no discord, war, envy, selfishness, greed, and protectionism. Thus, the only solution for our world is in the coming of our Lord Jesus Christ and his total reign. The church, his body, is expected to share in the reign of Jesus her Lord. In the meantime, however, she has to live in the world without being of the world and sharing its evil deeds. We, then, enter into the new millennium expecting the coming of our Lord who will give peace to his world and creation. Amen. Come, Lord Jesus.